Also by Gregory E. Buford
Making Ghosts Dance

kept

An American Househusband in india

Gregory E. Buford

KEPT: AN AMERICAN HOUSEHUSBAND IN INDIA by Gregory E. Buford

ISBN-13: 978-0999302811
ISBN-10: 0999302817
LCCN: 2018904794

Cover and interior designed by Ellie Searl, Publishista®

Visit the author's website at gregorybuford.com.

Moontower Press
Austin, Texas

This book is dedicated to my daughter, Nina Theekshana,
and my nephew, Benjamin Edward.

CONTENTS

Contents

PROLOGUE

I GAPE AT THE MAN in tears on the roof of our two-story home. From my vantage point I have the unspeakable misfortune of being able to see directly up his skirt-like *lungi* as he teeters on the edge, apparently ready to jump. A small army of security guards, domestic servants, turbaned laborers, and unknown passersby stand next to me, all come to witness this bizarre spectacle, many clearly hoping for action.

"Somebody, do something!" I demand, looking hopefully at our contract security guard.

He grins.

Biting my tongue and feeling a little guilty for thinking "either get it over with or get off my roof," I mount the ladder. If this guy jumps, it's going to mean some serious paperwork. As I climb, I can't help but wonder how this happened, how I got here, and what I did to deserve this. Whose idea was this anyway?

MY WIFE, DANA, WORKS FOR the US Department of State as a Foreign Service officer. Foreign Service officers are our nation's career diplomats. After passing a grueling exam, these gifted people are indoctrinated in Washington, DC, before being sent to one of the hundreds of US embassies and consulates around the world to issue visas to foreign nationals, attend cocktail parties, carry communiqués to foreign governments, host cocktail parties, assist Americans abroad, go to cocktail parties, and represent the American government outside the US. Did I mention the cocktail parties?

There are many civil service employees at the State Department in Washington who are not Foreign Service officers, and they don't typically get assigned abroad. And a relatively small number of Americans posted to American embassies and consulates around the world work for the military or other agencies, such as the US Agency for International Development, the CIA, the Department of Alien Invasion, and even the IRS.

For the most part, however, Americans working in US embassies and consulates abroad are Foreign Service officers working for the Department of State. Dana did not really want to be a diplomat. She was perfectly happy remaining in Texas, but that was not to be. And, as she is fond of pointing out, that was my fault. I, on the other hand, had wanted to be a diplomat for years, but that career was not to be, and that, too, was my fault.

Of course, I blame my parents. My mother grew up in a tiny town in East Texas and went to Stephen F. Austin State University— Axe 'em, Jacks! Since the university wouldn't allow young women to study accounting at that time, she got a bachelor's degree in music and a master's in education. Then, wanting to get as far from East Texas as possible, she took a job with the Department of the Navy and wound up as an elementary school teacher on US Naval Base Subic Bay in the Philippines. She traveled in Asia, and her fond memories of that time became the soundtrack of my childhood— always there in the background. My father, for his part, encouraged me to participate in the local Lion's Club Youth Exchange Program, which sent me to Belgium for a summer at the age of seventeen. I spent that summer with my host family's eighteen-year-old tooling around Europe in an ancient Peugeot, trying to figure out which country had the best-looking girls. (Results were inconclusive, but we had a *great* deal of fun.)

So it's no surprise to my parents when, one semester before my own graduation from Texas A&M University—Gig 'em, Aggies!— I open a book left on a table in the library that suggests amazing things to do my first year out of college. The first page offers work on a kibbutz in Israel.

I throw a wad of paper at my roommate, Javier. "Dude, what's a kibbutz?"

"Dude, I have no idea. I think it's a sandwich."

"Yeah, whatever, dude." (We say "dude" *a lot*.)

I turn the page: Teach English in Japan. I only need to be a native speaker of English—check—and have a college degree—almost check. I sign up. I go to the interview in Houston, where I get the name of the Japanese prime minister wrong.

"Dude," I tell Javier when I get back to the dorm, "If I get this job, I'm going to Japan."

"Man, you'll meet some girl and back out."

"No! Even if I meet the girl I'm going to marry, I'm going."

"OK, dude, whatever."

I shake Javier by the shoulders. "Seriously, dude. Don't let me let some stupid girl screw this up. Seriously!"

"Whatever, dude. Whatever you say."

Then I meet the girl I'm going to marry: Dana. And then I get my letter of acceptance from the Japan Exchange and Teaching Program.

I meet Dana under a tree on campus. "Uh, you remember that Japan thing I talked to you about."

"Yeah…"

"Well, uh, like…I sort of got, like, accepted."

"You *sort of* got accepted?"

"Yeah. And I, like, really want to go. In fact, I, uh, kind of promised myself that I'm going. That even if, uh, I met the girl I was going to marry…well, I've kind of always wanted to do something like this, and, uh, if I don't go, I feel like I'll kind of regret it for the rest of my life."

"Well," Dana says casually, "then I guess I'm going with you."

So, just like that, the deal is sealed. Well, not exactly "just like that," but that's the gist. We spend the first three years of our marriage teaching English and traveling all over Japan and the rest of Asia on a shoestring. We ski the Japan Alps, travel by ferry to

South Korea, take a slow boat to China on Christmas Eve, island-hop in Thailand, and visit Hong Kong, my mom's favorite city in the world. In Japan I meet a young German who has just been accepted into his country's diplomatic corps, and he tells me all about it.

"Wow. I want to be a diplomat someday," I tell Dana, fascinated, but I have other things to do first.

CHAPTER 2: BABY GAGA

IN 1995 WE MOVE BACK to the US, where Dana supports me financially and otherwise while I inexplicably attend graduate school in a suburb of Phoenix, Arizona. The whole time we are there I can't help but wonder how Phoenix even happened. I can just imagine pioneers traveling across the land in their covered wagons.

Amaziah: "Honey, why don't we just stop here and call this home?"

Imogene: "Duh. It's desert."

Amaziah: "Right."

Imogene: "Seriously? There's nothing but cactus and sand."

Amaziah: "Exactly."

Imogene: "OK. Sounds like a plan."

And thus, Phoenix was born.

I promise Dana we'll move back to Texas after I graduate so she can attend graduate school at the University of Texas—Hook 'em, Horns! As my life is committed to Arizona and then Texas for the next several years, I give up my dream of traveling the world as a US diplomat and get to work studying, finding a job, and having a baby. Technically, Dana does the having-a-baby part, but I am present (at both beginning and end). And it's a good thing too, because the doctor is conspicuously absent until the last twenty seconds or so, when she shows up to take credit. What a job!

Cole is born shortly before final exams of my last semester in graduate school. We had read all the fashionable books, attended the childbirth classes, and bought all the latest equipment—not all that lime-green lead-covered death-trap stuff our parents had so ignorantly used. We knew what to expect when we were expecting, by God, and thirty seconds after his birth I have him wrapped in one of my shirts—the books said he'd learn my smell—arguing with the nurses over whether or not he ought to be taken to the sterile, impersonal nursery or remain there in my loving arms.

Cole is beautiful despite the fact that, like all newborns, he bears no small resemblance to a frog, and I'm not about to let the nurses have their way with him. Convinced they'll carelessly switch him with the baby "Bradford" in the next room, I'm not taking any chances.

We—OK, mostly me—are traumatized when Cole doesn't jump right on the ol' nippy and begin nursing right away. Will he survive the night? I swear he's already losing weight, and Dana swears that if I tweak her nipples again to help him latch on, she's going to brain me. After I go to the nurses' station and apologize, I find myself banished from the room while they help Dana nurse Cole back from the brink of starvation.

"First-time dad," the nurses whisper as they exchange knowing glances. I bite my tongue and get a candy bar for supper.

Cole somehow survives the hospital and begins life with us at home.

My parents arrive in Phoenix only an hour after Cole's birth, because two days earlier they had jumped in the car and driven from Texas, hoping they would get lucky. They simply smile and watch as we—again, mostly me—obsess over every tiny detail of baby care and do everything wrong the first time. They never offer advice but are quick to give it when asked. They don't even complain when I wake up the whole house, calling the doctor because Cole hasn't dirtied a diaper in two days. (Note to new parents: If you are trying cloth diapers, do yourself a favor and give them up now! You will, sooner or later, anyway. We gave it a shot until we figured out our son would sleep *twice as long at night* in disposables. So go plant some offset trees and get some much-needed sleep.)

Contrary to popular opinion, graduate school is a great time for us to have a kid. After Cole's arrival, Dana works in the afternoons at the school's financial aid office, and I attend classes in the mornings. In this way, we both can take care of Cole half a day; she nurses him in the mornings, and I feed him from a bottle in the afternoons. We both get our Cole fix, and everything is peachy. Yet parenthood and graduation introduce me to an as-yet unfamiliar notion: I must *provide*. My life soon becomes consumed with the search for a job, and I am getting nowhere. Dana wants to go to graduate school in Austin, but I can't even get an interview there. Finally, we load everything in a U-Haul and head back to Texas, where at least we can bum off of family.

After a brief but painful stint living with Dana's parents—for the record, I'm eternally grateful—we lease a dumpy apartment a few blocks away from, statistically, the most dangerous intersection in Austin while I continue to look for a job. At last, I land a lousy sales job with MCI that pays the bills but not much more. The day I start working there I begin my search for something better. For a year I stalk a manager at Austin-headquartered PC giant Dell. Finally, he gives up and hires me. On my first day, he introduces me as the most persistent person he has ever met.

Life improves. We get the car fixed; it reeks of gasoline so badly that we have to drive with the windows down. We are ready to move;

obviously drunk men wander our apartment complex asking for handouts. We can stop paying for Dana's schooling with student loans. We no longer buy the mystery meat labeled "reduced for quick sale." Immediately, we move into a rental in a more wholesome neighborhood, and within several months we buy a little yellow house with "potential."

Cole turns two and is obviously brilliant. We shower upon him the attention it is the good fortune of all first children to get, and he repays us with good behavior. He really is an easy, well-behaved child, and I smugly tell myself this is the obvious result of superior parenting. A lot of one-child parents harbor the same ridiculous delusion.

When we move to Austin, Dana starts school and I start working. Cole has to go to day care. This devastates me. I fume over the injustice of it all, fretting aloud to Dana about the long-term effects of his not being with us all day, all the time. Every day, I flee work as early as politically possible and race across town to pick him up, cursing at every slow driver and racked with guilt.

Dana says I have a penchant for high drama. I won't even consider leaving Cole with my in-laws for a night so we can go out on the town. I essentially make it impossible for Dana and me to have any time alone at all, and I drive her nuts with my bellyaching. There has to be a way out of the rat race we are in, but if there is, I don't know it. In this day and age, this is just what we have to do: two incomes, kids in preschool from day one, work forever, and die. It never occurs to me there are any options.

As Dana nears completion of graduate school, the idea of the Foreign Service surfaces again. I'm making good money at Dell, but I am not content. I long for our carefree days teaching English in Japan, traveling and eating weird stuff like fish eyes and *natto*. (If the smell doesn't make you puke, you're sure to love it.) It isn't just me; we both have itchy feet, but Dana can live with normal. I need something more exciting. Yet we have a toddler and hope to have another bun in the oven soon. It looks like the days of youth hostels and backpacks are over.

"Is that all there is?" I croon, channeling my inner Peggy Lee. (I get this gene from my mother.) "Should we just buy a minivan and give up?"

One night, shortly before her graduation, after a day spent listening to me gripe about my job, Dana makes me a deal. She tells me to take the Foreign Service exam. If I pass, fine; I can tell my boss to shove his Q4 target, and she'll go with me overseas. If I don't pass, no harm done; I can tell my boss how excited I am about his Q4 target. Great! Even though we have just bought the little yellow house, I happily sign up for the test and eventually convince Dana that she might as well take it herself.

"Why not?" she says. Dana doesn't want to find herself overseas without a job.

We both consider it highly unlikely that Dana will pass the Foreign Service exam. Although Dana likes to travel, she is not particularly knowledgeable of or interested in foreign affairs. We agree, however, that I have a decent chance since I totally geek out on international anything and was a teaching assistant for International Political Economy class in grad school—seriously nerdy stuff. To our happy surprise, a few months later we both pass the written phase of the exam and immediately began preparing ourselves for the grueling day-long oral phase.

We drive to New Orleans to take the oral examination in an office space the State Department has leased for the occasion. The day before the big event, I have my first Bloody Mary at Commander's Palace—and realize they make me want to vomit— and we stuff ourselves with beignets at Café du Monde while trying not to think about our reason for being in town. We have spent months preparing for what, by all accounts, will be a harrowing experience: an entire day of mental punishment for the privilege of possibly being selected to be a US diplomat.

On the appointed day, we start at Mother's with the breakfast special for me—eggs, baked ham, grits, toast, juice, and milk—and a crawfish étouffée omelet for Dana before waddling down the street to the exam site. We are told to wait in a hallway with a half-dozen visibly nervous, clean-cut hopefuls in their brand-new suits and heavily gelled hair. One guy shows up half an hour late in jeans and a T-shirt. We wait until our names are called, one by one.

A man who looks like my father—dashing, handsome—ushers me into an undecorated room, where I wait alone with three metal chairs. I search for hidden cameras, wondering if I am being watched and whether my behavior alone in this room, with just my chair friends, is part of the test. I decide to sit and not move. After an eternity, two men arrive looking highly unamused, and the oral exam takes place almost exactly like this:

"We're going to ask you some questions. We will stop you when your answer has reached the time limit."

"Shoot."

"You're a Foreign Service officer in a small, underdeveloped Latin American nation. You're the only officer on duty on a Sunday when you receive a call stating a tour bus full of American senior citizens operating in a remote area has plunged off a road into a ravine one hundred feet below. What do you do?"

"Call the local police!"

"They are uncooperative."

"I call the tour bus company to get a list of passengers."

"You've got the list. Now what?"

"I contact the families of the injured."

"Injured? I didn't say there were any injured. Maybe you should contact the local hospitals to find out about any injuries."

"Yeah, I do that first. Contact the hospitals."

"Good idea, but all the phones are dead due to flooding in the area."

"Then I drive to the area personally and check with the hospitals."

"Roads have become impassable. Remember the flood?"

"I take the next flight."

"Airport is closed."

"I rent an ultralight, and, taking my satellite phone with me, I fly into the area and land on the roof of the local hospital, not forgetting to pack a week's worth of food and water and plenty of medical supplies. A riot having just broken out in the street below, I rappel down the side of the building and enter through a second-floor window, where I learn that Communist guerrillas have just taken the crash survivors hostage. I then radio for a helicopter to—"

"Mr. Buford, you are out of time. Thank you."

And things basically go downhill from there.

The examiners never ask me anything about foreign affairs; they don't care about my overseas experience; they don't want me to demonstrate my language skills; they aren't interested in my master's degree; they don't consider my work experience; they don't even ask me the name of the speaker of the Iranian parliament. Somebody, *please* ask me the name of the speaker of the Iranian parliament! (It was Hashemi Rafsanjani, for what it's worth.) I fail the exam miserably. Meanwhile, proving God has an excellent sense of humor, my wife is in the next room, passing with flying colors.

CHAPTER 3: A PASSAGE TO INDIA

WE THEN WAIT SEVERAL MONTHS—remember, this is the government we're talking about—and Dana finally gets a job offer from the State Department almost one year to the day after we bought the little yellow house. During these months of waiting, our lives have moved on, and now we aren't as gung-ho about the Foreign Service as we once were. For one thing, it was I who had really wanted to be a diplomat, not Dana. What am I going to do overseas? Write a book? Furthermore, I have a new and better boss, Dana has a standing job offer in Austin, Cole really seems to love his school as much as I hate dropping him off there every day, and we have just landscaped the yard.

Or rather, *I* have just landscaped the yard. Because, you see, my wife is a sexist pig. Since the day we married, I've shared equally with her those tasks in a home traditionally performed by wives for the last hundred thousand years, or so. I know what you're thinking: Greg has no idea how many millions of details his wife takes care of while he floats around, a clueless fumbler like most men, watching ESPN and eating chips off his chest. He never wonders how his socks get off the floor, who puts the extra pair of underwear in his son's preschool bag, who schedules dinner with the Balderramas and performs other "emotional labor" done almost exclusively by women. Well, I don't watch ESPN—Dana is obsessed—and I am telling the truth!

Seven days after we got married, Dana and I moved to Japan together, where, wallowing in newlywed bliss, we didn't think about any of this stuff. We had no kids, we both had jobs, we had (to us) plenty of money, and we slept on the floor on a twin-size futon. Our apartment was so small that we had to roll up the futon and stick it in a closet during the day so we could walk around. What problems could we possibly have? Dedicated to gender equality in every aspect of our marriage, we understood implicitly our superiority over more traditional couples, who seemingly had no qualms about living in the Stone Age. If we had never had kids, owned property, or bought a car, perhaps we would still be living in that fairy-tale world in which no one ever gets tired or throws a pair of scissors between her husband's legs.

Then we have a kid. And buy a house. We get credit cards and a yard and a vehicle. While I am still doing my share of household duties, other little jobs, such as car maintenance, yard work, and home repairs, nudge their way into our lives. Stupidly, I assume that, since we have always shared chores *inside* the home, Dana will step up to the plate when it comes to tasks that have traditionally been a man's domain. Why do I have to be the one to take the car to the shop? Only a moron would argue that I know more about cars than Dana.

Embarrassed by our yard (pictured), which resembles the surface of Mars, I alone and very inexpertly landscape it while grumbling to myself about my intention to spend the rest of our marriage on the couch watching ESPN. A pathetic attempt at landscaping, it is, but an attempt nevertheless. Once I finish, however, I am so bent out of shape at going it alone that I refuse to set foot in the yard again, and everything dies. Now, how's that for stubborn? (This gene comes from both my mother's and my father's sides.)

"I'm not making you do the yard because you're a man," Dana explains. "If I were a lesbian and married to a woman, I still wouldn't work in the yard."

This is supposed to make me feel better? "But you're not lesbian, so it's a *prima facie* case of sexual discrimination," I cry.

"God, you're such a nerd."

Luckily, Dana's offer from the State Department arrives just in time to keep us from being reported to the homeowners association. She's expected to report immediately to Washington, DC, for training, and I encourage her to take the job.

"I can take the exam again next year and maybe even pass," I tell her, "but let's don't wait."

"But the house, your job, Cole's school, my job offer? What about all that?" she asks.

In the end, it isn't all that difficult to convince Dana to go. Since she passed the exam, she's been captured by the mystique of the

Foreign Service. She's read personal accounts of diplomatic life and talked to former Foreign Service officers who have sold her on the idea of an exotic lifestyle as an American diplomat in a foreign land. With a somewhat vague idea of what we are getting into and little discussion of how long we might want to do it, Dana accepts the offer of employment with my blessing.

We feel special when the State Department sends movers—no stuffing everything into a U-Haul ourselves this time—for the move to an apartment in Falls Church, Virginia, a suburb of Washington, DC. I set up my office in the living room of our new apartment, because, to our great joy, Dell has agreed to let me try a new thing called "telecommuting." Although we pay for a full day of preschool, on most days I pick up Cole at noon and let him stay home with me the rest of the day. More than once, I take a multi-gazillion-dollar client call in the middle of a nasty diaper change or similar fun event.

The city of Falls Church has little to offer except proximity to the Foreign Service Institute and lots of tacky strip malls. It can, however, lay claim to Seven Corners, possibly the nation's worst intersection, an incomprehensible tangle of no less than seven major roads—and a lot more than seven corners—and their associated access roads that takes about twenty minutes to negotiate in the best of times. At the risk of being held in secret indefinitely at the whim of the president, I will admit that I sometimes have vivid fantasies of dropping a giant bomb on the whole mess so Falls Church can just start over.

Dana has to spend six long weeks in training before we will learn the location of her first assignment. She is taught to stand when an ambassador enters the room, how not to blow the cover of CIA agents, and how to think like a bureaucrat—i.e., inside the box. About a week into her training, we are given a list of more than one hundred cities where the US has either embassies or consulates. There is only one US embassy in a country, and it is always in the capital; there can be several US consulates in a particular country, and they function much like branch offices of the embassy. We are given one week to choose twenty cities from the list. We are told we can be sent to any city on our list but that we won't be sent anywhere not on our list—and we'll be there for *two years*.

I have a pretty good knowledge of geography, but I'm not familiar with many of these cities. There are places like Port Moresby (stay home after dark); Windhoek (one of Africa's best-kept secrets); Phnom Penh (rebels active in the countryside); and Ouagadougou (pronounced "wa ga doo goo"), capital of Burkina Faso, if that helps. There is no Rome, Paris, or even Tokyo. Since a great many of the posts on the master list are, to be undiplomatic, hellholes, choosing twenty places we can stomach is quite a challenge.

On the last day of her basic training, Dana's class of new Foreign Service officers and their spouses gather for the "flag ceremony," during which we will get our assignments. We literally sit on the edges of our seats until, near the end of the ceremony, we hear, "Dana Williams!"

Polite applause. Dana stands. A flag is held up. It looks familiar, but I can't quite place it. We turn to each other.

"Chennai," the speaker announces enthusiastically.

"Ch-what?" Dana asks me.

"Chennai."

"Where's that?"

"I forget." I feel a strong sense of buyer's remorse. I didn't talk Dana into this so we could go someplace I'd never heard of.

"India," someone whispers. We sit for a long time in silence.

After the ceremony, everyone mills about outside, either high-fiving one another or looking depressed. We are stunned. My parents made me promise to call them as soon as we got the assignment that would take us far away. They are not at all thrilled at the idea of us traipsing off to Timbuktu, or the like, with their grandchild, who has just turned three.

I call my mother on my mobile.

"Well, we found out where we're going," I say nervously, bracing myself.

"You're going to India, aren't you? I know you're going to India."

"Yeah, that's where we're going."

"Bye." She hangs up.

The next day I call my boss.

"You're doing *what*? You're going *where*? Are you nuts?"

Perhaps. In the end, he gets over it and secures me a position with Dell India, including a promotion and a fat raise. I am thrilled. Knowing I have a job waiting for me in India makes the move much more palatable.

The reality of what we are doing sinks in deep over the next few weeks as we say good-bye to family, get vaccinations for everything on the planet, and stock up on the necessities of life—strangely, to Dana, this means Pop-Tarts—that can't be readily found in India. We want Cole to start pre-kindergarten soon. Is there a good school in Chennai? Guess we should've thought of that earlier. Our doctor lectures us on disease prevention.

"They call dengue 'breakbone fever,' because that's what it feels like. Like all your bones are breaking at once."

"Okay. We'll take the vaccine for that," I say.

"Sorry. There's not one. Just don't get bit by any mosquitoes. And then, of course, there's malaria."

"Of course. All right, we'll take the shot for that one."

"There's no vaccine, per se, but you can take some medicines that *might* help. Of course, they all have very serious side effects."

"Of course."

"Best thing is to not get bit by any mosquitoes."

So, with no plan beyond spending the next two years in India and no idea how long Dana might stay in the Foreign Service and what that might mean for our family, my long-term career prospects, and our child's education, we say good-bye to the suburbs of Washington, DC, on a bitterly cold, rainy day and head to Amsterdam. (It takes so long to get to India—flight time: twenty-seven hours, fifty-five minutes—that the State Department allows us to stop in The Netherlands.)

Amsterdam is a beginner tourist's paradise: It's clean and safe, and everyone above the age of three speaks perfect English. An impeccably clean Mercedes taxi takes us to our hotel, and we lay over in the city for a couple of nights on our way to India. The food is good, the beer is better, and we wonder if this might be our last decent meal for a while.

We have rock-bottom expectations going to India. And I mean *rock-bottom*. For years, we have heard horror stories of the poverty, disease, super-spicy food, etc., that lay in wait for us there. We have read all the guidebooks, we went to the State Department's pre-departure orientation, we watched a Bollywood movie, and we have eaten at Bombay Palace several times. We had actually tried to go to India several years before while living in Japan, but just before we were to leave, there was an outbreak of bubonic plague, and our flight was cancelled. (Yes, that's right, bubonic plague. Like the kind that killed everyone in Europe a million years ago or so.)

We ended up going to Thailand instead. And, since that original attempt to visit the subcontinent, we've put a lot of travelers' miles on our shoes, riding buses across rural China, volunteering in Philippine slums, shoe-stringing it through Thailand, and more. In short, though we are seasoned travelers, we have a healthy respect for the challenges awaiting us in India; we understand India operates on a whole different level.

We arrive in India late on January 1, 2000. A few days earlier, I had been listening to alarmists on NPR speak of the doom looming with the Y2K computer glitch. (Does anybody remember that? It sure helped us sell a few computers at Dell!) The world is coming to an end, and it will be especially painful in developing countries unprepared for the change. I must admit I briefly question the wisdom of arriving in India on New Year's Day. As far I can tell, nothing goes amiss (that wasn't already scheduled to go amiss).

We change planes in India's capital, New Delhi, on the way to our final destination, and, as we come off the plane, Dana recognizes former Ohio governor and American ambassador to India, Richard Celeste, waiting for us. Eek! Dana stiffens and, using her best State Department regulation handshake, greets the ambassador, thanking him heartily for coming all the way out to the airport to welcome us to India and assuring him that this gesture is entirely unnecessary though greatly appreciated, etc., etc.

"Yes, yes, excuse me just a moment, Dana," Ambassador Celeste says, looking past us. "Honey! Honey! Over here, sweetheart," he shouts, waving, and a young lady runs into his outstretched arms. The ambassador turns again to us and says, "Dana, I'd like you to meet my daughter. I came out to the airport to welcome her to India too."

With that, he leaves us standing there looking down at our feet.

A few months later, Dana has the opportunity to travel to the American Embassy in New Delhi for training, and, in an embassy-wide staff meeting, the ambassador personally introduces Dana to the group by telling, to everyone's great amusement, the story of their first meeting.

CHAPTER 4: FLAME-SEX MARRIAGE

A S DANA, COLE, AND I LEAVE the relative civility of the Chennai airport, tropical humidity hits us like a brick to the head. Despite the late hour, a mass of humanity besieges the exit, shouting, expectorating and hawking its wares and services. An elderly woman with bloody stumps for hands begs us for food. A man tries to wrench our suitcases from my grasp. As I fight gallantly for our luggage, a foreign woman taps me on the shoulder.

"Uh, he's with us. I'm Nancy, your consulate sponsor."

Now burdened with our bags, the US consulate driver expertly mows a path through the crowd, leaving a rapidly diminishing wake in which we struggle to follow. Intense body odor, the essence of rotting garbage, and something being deep-fried in ancient oil accosts our senses. Cole, jet-lagged and cranky, clings to my leg like a dog in heat, his little eyes wide. A mustachioed police officer with a big stick and an even bigger belly snarls at the mob, and the path widens for us. We make a beeline for a white SUV with diplomatic plates, dive inside and lock the doors. Nancy turns to us from the front seat and says with a chuckle, "Welcome to India."

Curious faces press against the thick blast-proof glass. Multiple hands probe a half-open window. Nancy quickly rolls it up. Behind us, the driver loads our bags, stopping occasionally to shout at the dozen or so individuals who offer to help him in exchange for a tip. He allows none of these gentlemen to lay a hand on our stuff, but, nonetheless, they indignantly demand remuneration for their services as we speed away.

Under Nancy's comprehending gaze, we sit in stunned silence as the driver negotiates a potholed highway fringed with food stalls, squalid huts, and bullock carts. The clientele of some of the more popular roadside stalls spills into the streets, seemingly unaware of the danger of being flattened by one of the many grossly overloaded trucks roaring past.

Before long, we enter a leafy neighborhood of walled yards and uniformed security guards. Over walls topped with razor wire or shards of glass we can make out spacious mansions draped with climbing flowers. We pull into a gated compound and park under a carriage porch in front of a white two-story building. What looks like an extended Indian family stands on our new doorstep, grinning eagerly. We roll to a stop, and they noisily descend upon us.

Dazed by lack of sleep and our chaotic surroundings, we are unable to protest as our bags find their way to the front door, courtesy of our amiable welcoming party. Our sponsor comes with the key, and before I know what's happened, a rather large Indian woman is standing in our kitchen, asking what we'll want for breakfast. She tells me where to put our dirty laundry and asks if we need anything before turning in.

"Good night, Madam. Good night, Master," she says, leaving us to collapse in a heap.

"Who on earth was that?" Dana asks in the sudden stillness.

"Beats me." I groan. "Wait! Where's Cole?"

Roused from our stupors, we frantically search the house, only to find our son tucked in bed in his pajamas, snoring loudly.

✳✳✳

I wake up a few hours later wondering where I am and what time it is. This is not my familiar bed. The room smells alien. It is deathly quiet. My feet are tangled up in the mosquito net draped over us. Of course, I don't have a local mobile phone yet, so I fumble in the darkness for my watch. Where did I put it? Last night had been something of a blur.

"It's 4 a.m.," Dana says. She sounds wide awake. "I've been up for hours."

"Four o'clock? That would make it, like, 6:30 p.m. back in Virginia. No wonder we can't sleep."

We lie there until Cole starts crying and then bring him in bed between us. He is disoriented and grumpy—like me—and it takes us a few minutes to bring him up to speed.

"Remember? We're in India," Dana says.

Cole shakes his head. "No. I don't think so."

Shortly after dawn, the doorbell rings.

"Who on earth do you think that is?" I ask. I roll out of bed and pull on the clothes I'd thrown on the floor the night before. "I'll go check it out." Cole follows me downstairs in his underwear.

It is Selvi, the rotund lady who had taken charge of us the night before. She is lugging bags of groceries.

I rub my eyes. "Can I help you?"

"Time for breakfast," she says and pushes past me into the house.

"Uh, OK."

"Who is it?" Dana calls from upstairs.

"Selvi from last night," I yell back. "Apparently, she's going to make breakfast."

After a breakfast of cheese toast—"All American people are liking cheese toast," Selvi explains.—Cole and I explore our new digs.

Outside our new home's front gate, a gray tile set in the white perimeter wall reads "The Flame." Bright pink and purple bougainvillea partially obscures the barbed wire stretched along the length of the wall. Coconut palm and mango trees, draped with climbing elephant ear, shade a huge yard full of hibiscus, banana, azalea, and the occasional papaya. A trellis arch of bougainvillea straddles a circular driveway leading to a carriage porch and our front door.

"You know," I say appraisingly, "if we climb up on top of that"—the carriage porch—"we could throw water balloons down on people that come to visit us."

"Cool," Cole drawls.

Servants' quarters—a low, rambling structure—dominate our backyard. We wonder at an enormous generator that fills one room of this building, a device we will quickly learn is very handy during the periodic power outages. The two remaining rooms are available for housing servants and their families. There is also an Asian-style hole-in-the-ground toilet and a shower. I am shocked that people would willingly live under such conditions; I am stunningly naïve.

The Flame, like most homes of the wealthy in Chennai, is built on a concrete slab out of cinder blocks and mortar and painted a blinding white. Large and eccentric, the house has obviously been added on to several times. An interesting "secret passageway" connects the master bedroom with one of the other bedrooms, providing Cole an ideal setting for hours of "haunted house" and other adventures.

The house is high-ceilinged and full of light. The kitchen alone is larger than the apartment we lived in as newlyweds in Japan. The floors are an ugly composite stone tile except in the hexagonal living room, which has a wood parquet in dismal condition and a large pillar in the middle of it. Here and there, deafening A/C units are mounted in holes cut directly through the walls to the outside. In each room there are several apparently useless light switches on the walls that drive me nuts until I label the ones that actually operate something. Thick bars cover all windows, presumably for a reason.

Overall, we are quite happy with the house; it is a rather quirky mansion but certainly larger than the little yellow house we owned in the States. I claim a bright upstairs room for my home office from where I can keep an eye on what's going on outside. A long, narrow bedroom and bathroom at the end of an upstairs hallway will keep guests mercifully distant yet accessible. Each room is furnished with new government-issue furniture from North Carolina that seems out of place in our tropical home.

Around noon our consulate sponsor, Nancy, arrives to check on us. She tells us a story, almost certainly apocryphal, about our home's recent past. In The Flame lived a young househusband and his wife who worked at the consulate. A short distance away, in another consulate-owned home, christened "Love," lived a young housewife and her husband who worked at the consulate alongside the wife of the young househusband living in The Flame. Are you with me? The househusband and the housewife of their respective homes became friends and eventually lovers. In the meantime, the two worker bees likewise began having an affair.

After some time, all of these goings-on were discovered, and the four of them realized how silly their living arrangements were. The young housewife promptly moved into The Flame to be with her lover, and the other young lady moved into Love to be with her career-minded beau. As the story goes, one pair of the two eventually married and is still together. As for the other, they eventually drifted apart.

CHAPTER 5: WELCOME TO STRANGELAND

B Y DEFAULT, SELVI BECOMES OUR first domestic servant ever. Before I'd even gotten my head around this notion—domestic servitude—it's a *fait accompli*. The idea of having another person do our cooking, cleaning, and laundry offends, at some level, my progressive values, but I quickly change my tune when I see how much Selvi needs the job and—I must admit—what an affordable luxury it is for our family. By the time our first guest from the States arrives and indignantly says, "How can you sit on your butt while she waits on you?" I am defending the institution.

"Don't you do that when you go to a restaurant or a hotel?"

"Yeah, I suppose."

"And besides, we pay Selvi a good wage and treat her fairly."

Selvi wears a cheap blue or yellow sari to work every day that prominently displays the rolling folds of her great belly. (Though Indian women are quite modest in dress, that doesn't mean they can't leave their tummies hanging out. Go figure.) With the top of her head just reaching my chest, Selvi makes up in width for what she lacks in height. Conveniently, her location at any point in time can be ascertained by the agreeable jingling of her abundant bangles. When Selvi moves, she does so slowly, her ample hips swaying in an exaggerated fashion reminiscent of a ship on high seas. She wears a stone in her nose, and her face is more often than not tinged yellow by the application of turmeric powder as a kind of makeup. After she's been cooking and cleaning for several days, we guess that means we've hired her. She certainly doesn't ask.

Each time I speak to Selvi, she bobbles her head loosely from side to side, and I soon learn this is a common Indian gesture that confounds most foreigners. The head bobble is kind of like a nod except that, with eyes straight ahead, the head tilts rapidly from left to right instead of up and down. Since Selvi and other Indians seem to use this gesture to mean "yes," "no," and "maybe," it amounts to more ambiguity than I'm willing to accept from my household staff. After several major miscommunications involving the head bobble, I ask Selvi to answer with a clear verbal "yes" or "no," head bobble optional.

Selvi takes some getting used to. She claims she has worked for various occupants of The Flame for many years, but she can never seem to produce any proof of this when pressed. Her service in our employ reminds me of a child's windup toy that frantically bounces, hops, and kicks for a first few seconds but then quickly winds down and sputters out, making a final pathetic hop at the end of its life when coaxed. Selvi performs wonderfully for the first week in our home, but then her rate of deceleration is nearly comical. Soon, she needs to be prodded—no, not literally—to do anything. We wonder if we should let her go.

"Come on, Mr. Tough Guy. You can do it," Dana coaxes.

"No way. You do it."

"But she's terrible. I mean, she's nice, but she doesn't actually do anything."

"Fine," I say. "Then you fire her. I like her cheese toast."

"It's *inedible*. Seriously, you can't eat it."

In the end, we agree there's just something about Selvi. Something about the way she lacks even the most miniscule amount of initiative, something about her innocent obedience when I tell her to stop writing her name on the wall in our foyer, something about how she tries and fails to make edible cheese toast again and again. Finally, I guess we keep her because she makes us laugh.

✳✳✳

Dell has been kind enough to give me a month to transition to India, but Dana has to start work right away. Every day, she and several other young diplomats sit behind bullet- and blast-proof glass and interview Indian applicants for visas that will allow them to enter the US. If this doesn't make any sense to you, I'll explain it like this: We don't let everyone in. In fact, we don't even let most of them in. Mainly, we let in just the rich and well connected. Every single day, outside American embassies and consulates around the world, there are long lines of people who have been waiting since dawn for the privilege—for which they have to pay a substantial fee—of trying to convince a junior officer in the Foreign Service that, if they are granted a visa, they will return to their home country before their visa expires and not remain illegally in the US. All Foreign Service officers are required to participate in this stressful, thankless dues-paying assignment for at least one tour of duty. These interviews take place at breakneck speed, lasting less than two minutes, and in Chennai the five visa officers perform several hundred each day. A much larger number of applicants are not interviewed in person; they are either issued a visa or not based upon submitted documents.

(After 9/11, when investigations determined that most of the 9/11 hijackers were never interviewed when they applied for a visa, visa officers around the world surely thought, "Of course not. We don't interview the vast majority of applicants, and this has been policy for years." Nevertheless, Mary Ryan, Assistant Secretary of State for Consular Affairs, with overall responsibility for visas and a shining star within the department, got the axe, and from that point forward all visa applicants have been interviewed, albeit at an even faster speed. At any rate, any Foreign Service officer will tell you there is no possible way he or she can identify a potential terrorist via a two-minute interview at a visa window.)

While Dana is slinging visas, Cole and I hang around the consul general's pool, lazing in the sun and gorging on fresh tropical fruit. The consul general is the person in charge at a consulate, and he or she reports directly to the ambassador at the embassy in the capital. The consul general in Chennai has a spacious residence on the banks of the Adyar River, complete with swimming pool and tennis court. We will soon learn that in the summer months the Adyar stinks of raw sewage and that stench will provide the backdrop for many diplomatic functions, such as the consulate's Fourth of July celebration.

While Cole and I enjoy the time we spend together, reality is creeping up on us. I'm expected to begin working soon, and Cole has to go to school. Dana and I decide it's better to send Cole to preschool for half a day at the American International School of Chennai than to leave him home for the entire day with a nanny. Cole will finish school at noon and remain home in the afternoon, where I will be working out of my office and can keep an eye on the situation as needed. We'll need to hire someone to mind Cole in the afternoon while I work, and I dread the task.

Selvi swears she can handle Cole as well as her other duties, but we aren't quite sure since, in our opinion, she isn't exactly succeeding in her primary role. It's not that Cole won't be safe; we just know Selvi isn't exactly going to engage him in educational activities. Furthermore, Selvi is completely incapable of telling Cole "no." If Cole so much as sighs, she looks as if she's going to burst an artery. She fawns over him completely and refuses to believe that we don't want to give him anything and everything he wants all the time since, as Americans, we must be able to afford it. If we let her have full rein, his feet will never touch the ground again.

For his part, Cole doesn't know what to make of the idea of domestic help; he can't yet understand Indian English, and Selvi doesn't speak American Toddler. Cole marvels that Selvi comes shuffling at the push of a button—and is put out when we won't let him use said button. He wonders aloud if Selvi is one of Dana's sisters. My tall, thin, redheaded wife finds this idea quite amusing. We simply tell Cole Selvi has a job, just like any other job one gets paid to do.

So I instruct Selvi to put the word on the street that we are looking for an English-speaking nanny and that I will be interviewing the next morning. Anyone who employs servants in India knows the fastest and most reliable way of disseminating news is to let it hit the servants' grapevine, and, as I fully expect, a line of women waits outside our gate early the next day. We hire a tall woman named Heather, who has most of her teeth and happens to be the product of a British father and Indian mother. As a native speaker of English, Heather can communicate with us perfectly, giving her an edge over the competition.

Strangely, at the end of her interview and having already been told she has the job, Heather leans close and whispers, "I am Christian."

"Heather," I say, also in a whisper, "I don't care if you're the Pope. Do your job, and we won't have any trouble." With that, she leaves.

We soon learn of Heather's fondness for frequently pointing out that her adherence to Christianity makes her superior to the other servants in every way. This "holier than thou" attitude rubs me the wrong way from the start, and I'll later find that I would have done well to have heeded my instincts.

Meanwhile, the electricity is going out almost daily, and I enjoy my first experience with the Indian medical system. Well, I take that back. What I experience certainly does not resemble in any way what the average Indian goes through with an ear infection, but, as expatriates, we qualify as the lucky few. For six US dollars, the doctor makes an hour-long house call at my convenience, and the pharmacy delivers my prescription medication free of charge. To say "prescription" is not entirely correct, as I simply call the pharmacy and they deliver what I want, no questions asked. As it turns out, buying cheap Indian equivalents of ridiculously expensive American prescription drugs will become a favorite pastime of our guests from the US, so much so that we begin dealing directly with a wholesaler for all our visitors' medicinal needs.

We are coping with other aspects of life in India as well. At the closest thing in Chennai to a supermarket, barefoot children compete to carry our bags to the car. It breaks my heart, and I tip them. I don't know if it's the right thing to do—they should be in school—but they are providing a service and earning money to feed their families. Am I condoning child labor or simply acknowledging their reality and supporting them where they are?

We also learn that no working-class Indian person will ever say no to any request from us. It doesn't matter if what we ask is utterly impossible; the answer is always yes, even if everybody involved understands the answer should clearly be no. For example, I ask a repairman when he will have our washing machine fixed.

"Tomorrow, saar."

The guy's already told me he will have to order parts. "Tomorrow? Is that possible?"

The man bobbles his head, leaving me wondering what he means.

"I'm sorry. Is that a 'yes' or a 'no'?"

"Yes, saar. It will be done."

"Are you sure?"

"Yes, saar!" His head bobbles wildly.

"I mean if you can't do it by tomorrow, just let me know."

"It will be done, saar."

"You do understand that the motor inside the machine exploded?"

"Yes, saar." Head bobble.

"But that's no problem?"

"No problem, saar."

"Suppose I took the machine and pushed it off a cliff. Could you fix it tomorrow?"

"No problem, saar." Head bobble. "It will be fixed."

"What if I push it off a cliff and bury it twelve feet under a large block of solid granite?"

"It will definitely be done tomorrow, saar."

At this point I have to look away, because his gyrating head is giving me motion sickness.

We work on getting driver's licenses, a bank account, internet, cable TV, etc., in order to make life in India as normal as possible for us. Most types of paperwork necessary for these sorts of things require that a female applicant give either her father's or husband's details, as well as her own. This does not sit well with my wife. Thinking of the time I spent alone in the yard, landscaping the little yellow house, I pat Dana on the head and say, "Well, don't you worry your little head about it, sugar. Let me fill that out." As a silent protest against this blatant sexual discrimination, she most often writes "Donald Duck" in the box labeled "If female applicant, include father's or husband's name," and I support her wholeheartedly in this courageous act of civil disobedience.

We learn that anything can be delivered to the house, no matter how low its value, making it unnecessary to go anywhere to make a purchase; it's like Amazon Prime before it was a thing. When I need a mobile phone, three young men come to The Flame and spend two excruciating hours demonstrating the features of their entire product line. A representative from our internet service provider stays so long that I have to ask him to leave. I never need go to an ATM for cash; the bank dispatches a courier to deliver the dough.

We try to adapt to Indian business practices and etiquette, but simple things like calling Dana at the office can present a challenge. My first telephone conversation in India goes something like this:

"Good afternoon, American Consulate."

"Hello, may I speak to—"

"Hallo."

"Yes, may I speak to Dana—"

"Hallo!" Interrupted again.

"I would like to speak to—"

"Hallo!"

"Are you not able to hear me?"

"Hallo! Yes, I can hear you. Hallo!"

"Please stop saying 'hallo'!"

"I can hear you. Hallo!"

"Then why do you keep saying 'ha—"

"Hallo!"

"If you say 'hallo' again, I'm going to hang up."

"Hallo!"

I make it a point to call Dana's direct number next time.

CHAPTER 6: BETTER TO RE-GIVE THAN RECEIVE

OUR CONSULATE SOCIAL SPONSOR, NANCY, holds a small welcome party for us at her home, which is furnished with government-issue North Carolina furniture identical to ours.

"You know, I think we're going to like it in Chennai," I tell her. "I'm kind of getting used to the place."

It's true. Despite the air pollution, the filth, the poverty—OK, there are some things not to like—I'm finding the people, cultural differences, and Indian way of doing things fascinating. I feel as if I'm taking Anthropology 101 all over again. India is unbelievably exotic to my American eyes, each day full of mind-blowing experiences. For example, I run into members of the ancient community of eunuchs in India known as *hijra*, officially recognized in some South Asian countries as a third gender. Supposedly, these folks, who dress as women, are mostly born male. Then their man parts are removed at a young age by daily tightening a horse hair around them until they just drop off. See? Mind-blowing.

Nancy smirks. "Greenhorn, you're still in what I call the 'honeymoon' phase."

It's at Nancy's party that we meet Harish. His gravelly voice, roughened by years of overuse, and his understated yet imposing manner conjures for me visions of Marlon Brando, his mouth full of cotton, doing Don Corleone in *The Godfather*. Harish is the only non-consulate person invited to our welcome party, and he comes on as strong as raw garlic. We are immediately put off by his overbearing nature, yet one does not easily avoid Harish. He corners us and drops a long list of names of current and former consulate officials, adding how good a friend he is to each of them. Before we can ask who has let this guy into our party, we have somehow committed to joining him for dinner the following week; Harish does not take no for an answer.

The next morning, two men present themselves at our home, displaying Harish's business card. When I open the gate, the men bring in two large boxes. Before I can protest, one of them utters, "Gift from Harish-bai," and they are gone. The boxes contain small packages of no-name-brand frosted cornflakes, mango pickles, *barfi*—the world's most unfortunately named sweet—chewing gum and *chivda*—the Indian equivalent of Chex Mix—which we distribute among the staff.

"Bai", by the way, is an honorific suffix tacked onto a man's name, meaning "uncle." In India it is customary for children and young adults to address older men as "uncle" even when there is no blood relationship. When introducing a man several years older, someone may refer to a person as "my Uncle So-and-So." Older women are referred to as "aunts" and peers as "cousins," and so one can never be sure who is actually related to whom. Everyone calls our new friend "Harish-bai" as a means of demonstrating respect, as well as endearment.

Besides his overbearing manner, we have another reason to be wary of Harish. American Consulate employees often find themselves besieged during their personal time by people seeking US visas for themselves or their friends. As a Foreign Service officer, you might be approached by a beggar or hawker of souvenirs in the market, and, after you've refused his entreaties to help you lighten your wallet, he, as often as not, will ask if you can help him or his "cousin" obtain a visa. It doesn't stop there; waiters, businesspeople, elevator operators, microwave repairmen, and Hindu priests all have, or know someone who has, recently applied for or been denied a visa, and they aren't shy about asking for help. It gets to the point that we stop identifying ourselves as in any way related to the American Consulate. I begin introducing Dana as a housewife and myself as a swimsuit model, two equally unbelievable prospects. We wonder if Harish will begin asking Dana for help in getting his friends visas.

On the appointed night, Harish picks us up in a surprisingly junky un-air-conditioned Toyota Corolla and takes us to a modestly upscale restaurant where the parking lot attendant bows and scrapes as if Harish were an eleventh avatar of Vishnu himself. Harish floats regally through the door, where the huge wait staff assembles to greet us. A nervous manager in a cheap black suit ushers us to his "best table," alternately barking orders at his staff and beaming at us.

"They have prepared a special meal for me, but you can have anything you like," Harish says.

The manager shouts a command, at which the servers disappear in a frantic jumble of activity. A banquet for ten soon arrives for Dana and me to share: soup-like black lentil and kidney bean creamed *dal*; *biryani*, an elaborate rice and vegetable dish containing richly seasoned chunks of lamb flavored with saffron; tender lamb chops cooked in yogurt—or curd, as they call it in India—and exotic spices; a superb curry of red snapper; boneless, marinated chicken pieces roasted on a skewer in the high heat of a tandoori oven; *raita*—homemade yogurt with chopped tomato, cucumber, and red onion; various Indian breads, such as *chapatti*, *naan*, and *paratha*; and sweet *lassi*, a frothy drink of yogurt, water, and sugar that serves very well to moderate the heat of some of the spicier dishes. (Find a recipe for lassi on gregorybuford.com.) Harish touches none of it. He eats a simple dish of rice and plain *moong*—yellow lentil—dal. To the manager's great relief, we pronounce the meal fabulous. He formally introduces himself to us, pockets Dana's business card, and promises to take care of us during our time in Chennai. The bill for dinner never arrives at our table, and, when we ask Harish about this, he laughs and changes the subject.

On a subsequent visit without Harish, the same manager relentlessly pushes us to order more, particularly the more expensive items on the menu.

"I think you will need two orders of naan, saar. One is not enough."

I'm not buying it. "No, thanks. One is enough."

"And the prawns—please get the prawns. You will love them."

"No, that's all right."

With a careless bobble of the head: "I will make them for you. It is no problem," he says.

"No. No prawns."

"But you simply must have some more food. The fish. It is decided."

"No. No fish."

"Of course, saar." He turns to Dana. "Begging your pardon, madam, but could you please kindly help my cousin who is seeking a visa for study in your country?"

I've had enough. "Look. We like your food, but if you don't stop, we are never coming back. *And* I'm going to tell Harish-bai."

The man gasps, wide-eyed, his head bobbling frantically. Needless to say, he never hassles us again.

✽✽✽

Not long after we meet Harish, a small community of squatters moves onto the vacant lot next to our house. These are some of the most bedraggled, roughly hewn people I have ever seen, and they proceed to erect sturdy huts of grass, bamboo, and scrap wood. More and more of them come with their naked babies, who toddle in the street while Mom and Dad construct a roof for them to sleep under, until there are perhaps twenty people living there, not including young'uns.

Once, when Cole and I are out for a walk, one of these children, sitting bare-bottomed amid broken glass and gravel on the side of the road, smiles at us as we pass. Her hair is filthy and matted beyond redemption, with an orange tint—possibly a result of malnutrition. We stop to shake hands with her, but she runs shyly away and buries herself in her mother's sari. I guess she is about two and a half years old, but her mother tells me she is four—almost a year older than Cole, who towers over her. Not for the first time I consider how fortunate I am to have been born American, with access to free, quality education, to parents who had the wherewithal to feed and clothe me.

These folks turn out not to be squatters at all. Or, rather, they turn out to be legitimate squatters. They are itinerant construction workers who travel from site to site, making their homes where the work is for the moment. And for the moment, it is in the lot next to us. They continue working on their huts until they have three rather impressive shacks. They even tap into a power line somewhere— perhaps ours—and thus are able to burn a single bulb at night.

There is a dirt alley between the now not-so-vacant lot and our circular driveway. Therefore, as we come and go in our beautiful red Jeep Grand Cherokee, we can watch these people go about their day.

I marvel at how the women squat comfortably in positions that would render me unable to walk for hours as they slowly cook lunch or dinner over a fire made of anything they can find that will burn. For two years we drive past these people in the comfort of our air-conditioned SUV, gauge progress on the mansion they are building, put up with their noise, and even exchange pleasantries from time to time.

CHAPTER 7: DRIVING MISS CRAZY

MUCH TO MY DISMAY, THE TIME comes for me to go to work. I fly weekly to Dell India's headquarters in Bangalore. I'm happy to go to Bangalore because, as much as I love Indian food, I'm beginning to tire of eating it every single day, and Bangalore has something I can find nowhere else in India: Kentucky Fried Chicken. Or, rather, KFC, which you're supposed to call it since "the Colonel" decided the word *fried* was bad for his image and rebranded the company name. But let's face it: "fried chicken," which is what KFC sells, is actually "fried" and it is still "finger-lickin' good," even though they don't like to use that one anymore either. At any rate, when you've had nothing but Indian food for a couple of months, and you get an opportunity to go to KFC, you go and get the all-dark-meat four-piece dinner with biscuit, and you don't worry about whether the chicken is "fried" or just "F'd."

Since I am flying back and forth between Chennai and Bangalore, I have to relinquish a good deal of control over my little angel to Nanny Heather, who seems more or less all right. But will Heather wipe Cole's nose on her sari if she has no tissues? Will she read to him when I'm not there, or will she just stick him in front of the Evil One, the Other Parent, the Neglect-O-Matic all day to watch mindless garbage that will rot his young brain? Are career and money really worth this? No. But what choice do I have?

By the time I get back to the daily grind, our household staff has somehow ballooned to no less than *six* people getting in our way and trying to make themselves look busy without much success. I guess I try to compensate for my frequent absences by hiring a bunch of people to keep the house full and be there for Cole. What I soon realize is that having six people in our employ means I need a full-time manager just to keep track of them. You already met Selvi, who stood at the door when we first arrived. We finally get enough of her attempts at cooking and ask her to stick to housekeeping. She simply shrugs and takes another break.

I'm surprised to learn that Heather, the nanny, while fluent in her native English speaks almost none of the local Tamil language. She informs me that Tamil is "low class." Yes, the patina is rubbing off our relationship fast, and although I don't have any good reason for it, I don't trust her. Heck of a person to leave your child with all day!

There is Narayanan, the gardener, whom everybody calls Tata, which means Grandpa. We aren't sure how old he is, but, when he applies for the job, he produces the disintegrating remnants of letters of recommendation written by former occupants of The Flame itself, which prove that he worked there as "second boy" *prior to 1940*. I don't dare touch his ancient documents out of fear they might crumble to dust. To hear him tell it, life has been good to Narayanan. As a young man, he landed a plum job as gardener at the American Consulate, from which he has been retired for at least ten years.

Narayanan normally comes to work in a cotton *lungi*, the preferred dress of working-class Indian men. The lungi is essentially a colorful wrap-skirt that can be worn down to the ankles or hiked up and tied in a knot between the legs to function like shorts. Narayanan stands about four foot six, has a few teeth, and often delves into long discourses in Tamil, waving his arms about for emphasis and either not understanding or not caring that I have absolutely no idea what he is saying. All the other servants think he is cute. Me too. Excellent gardener.

Next comes a member of the "untouchable" class who won't tell me her name and whose job is to clean the toilets in the servants' quarters. I hire her one day after I naïvely think we have finally become fully staffed. I am annoyed to hear agitated voices wafting up the stairs to my office, my audience room to which all household disputes ultimately make their way. As if I don't have anything better to do, I march downstairs to dispense justice on the spot. It seems the bathroom in the detached servants' quarters has become unclean and foul-smelling, and, according to Indian custom, only *dalit* are "low" enough to clean the toilets of servants. It is okay for the servants to clean my toilets, just not their own toilets.

I instruct Selvi to find someone not too proud to clean the servants' bathroom and get that person to the house pronto. Within a few hours, a rather haggard woman is produced who agrees to come once a week and clean the toilets in the servants' quarters. I ask her name, but she only averts her eyes. I find the notion that this woman is destined by birth to perform disgusting work utterly repugnant, and so I decide to pay her more per hour than I pay the other employees, since she does a job no one else is willing to do. I keep that fact quiet so it won't cause trouble for her. This is my first firsthand experience with India's caste system, about which I had read and heard much, but it won't be my last.

Next, we actually hire a chauffeur, and it's the best money I ever spend. Driving in India is not exactly for the faint at heart, and, in fact, when you rent a car in India, it always comes with a driver attached. There should be a road sign for the benefit of newcomers: "You don't have to be crazy to drive in India, but it helps." Indeed, road rules seem merely conventions that a foreigner would have no way of knowing.

Hopelessly crowded, narrow streets filled with clueless pedestrians, sleeping cows, auto-rickshaws—India's ubiquitous three-wheeled mini-taxi—and stalls selling everything imaginable soon have the most laid-back non-Indian drivers on the verge of going postal. Each time I drive, within five minutes I'm either a nervous wreck or ready to kill somebody, and I don't need that kind of stress in my life. Virtually every expatriate we know employs a driver, and not just to drive but to provide security when the car is parked on the street, to run errands, to wash the car, and more.

For this job we hire the amazing Dinesh, twenty-five. He has little experience and few qualifications, but I like his smile. Dinesh is as close to the perfect employee that anyone is ever going to get: He comes to work on time, performs above the call of duty, and rarely asks for a loan. He always has a smile on his face, and he drives slower than my eighty-eight-year-old grandmother. I tell him to speed up, and he replies, "Yes, saar," and continues to drive safely and slowly. Typically, he washes the car once a day and spends the balance of his time detailing. He runs all our errands, makes an excellent babysitter and security guard, and is just altogether a good guy to have around.

I've never seen anyone look so proud to drive a car in my life as Dinesh on the day our car arrives from the US. There's a pecking order among drivers of the rich and famous in India. Basically, the better the car you drive, the higher your status. (This, of course, is not unlike what a fancy car does for its driver in any country.) Most cars in India are small white uncomfortable affairs with no distinguishing characteristics. As we appear to have the only bright-red Jeep Grand Cherokee on the subcontinent, Dinesh attains an almost godlike status among his fellow chauffeurs. Driving in crowded areas—essentially, everywhere—in our unusual vehicle, we create a mob-like situation. Gawking passersby stop what they are doing, surround the car, and press their faces against the glass. We cause an accident when a motorcyclist rear-ends a truck because he is staring at our car instead of watching the road. Thank goodness Dinesh is behind the wheel.

Finally, there is Leela, our cook, the woman we should never have hired. In fact, I'm not entirely sure why we did. Oh, now I remember. We couldn't stand any more of Selvi's cooking. Food means a lot to us, and Dana had a grand dream that we would be able to afford in India the services of a true chef, one who would whip up for us great culinary masterpieces for dinner every night. We would be summoned to the table without a care in the world, à la Downton Abbey—Indian-style—and all with fairness toward our workers. Well, it doesn't exactly work out the way Dana had planned.

Leela is in her sixties and wears thick glasses and the same yellow sari every day. She has Selvi's rotund figure, but, like Heather, Leela is Christian and, also like Heather, she believes this is proof of her superiority. Christian charity doesn't keep her from stealing from us, however, but we don't discover that right away. Leela arrives late every day, grumbles as a general rule, asks for a raise with irritating frequency, argues with the other servants, and is territorial about her kitchen with everyone, including me. She claims to pray for my happiness daily, which is probably the only thing that keeps me from strangling her. At any rate, after I tell her what to make and listen to her personal problems between calls from my boss in Singapore, Leela can bake a pretty good chicken.

The presence of this horde of servants in our house quickly has a not entirely unforeseen detrimental effect on Cole. He is a smart child, but it doesn't take a genius to figure out how the staff can easily be manipulated. My job as a parent is to raise a responsible, well-adjusted child without causing any major destruction along the way. On the other hand, our nanny and the rest of the household team want to keep Cole quiet and happy by any means necessary. Cole figures out in a hurry that making the slightest peep gets him anything he wants.

As you may guess, this doesn't sit well with me. Working out of my home office, I can hear everything going on downstairs, and I don't like what I hear. Sample conversation:

Cole: "I want that entire bag of Super-Gummy Maxi-Sugar Puffs!"

Heather (though it could be any one of the six): "I'm not sure a whole bag is a good idea, and you should ask nicely."

Cole: "Waaaaaaaaah!"

Heather: "Here! Take the whole bag, and there's more when you finish that."

At this point, I interrupt my work and intervene to keep my kid from becoming a spoiled, rotten brat and in the process undermine any miniscule authority Heather might have had in the first place. I tell our hired help that my child can be told no.

"Giving Cole everything he wants is not good for him," I explain.

"Yes, saar. Of course, saar," Heather says and then carries on as before.

Life in India is having positive effects on Cole, as well. He is fascinated by the different languages and learns he can be understood better by nonnative speakers of English if he talks clearly and succinctly. He learns to like a lot of South Indian cooking, and he can distinguish between a Hindu temple and a Muslim mosque. Cole attends school with children from Belgium, Korea, Japan, India, France, China, and Germany, and he learns to appreciate their differences. Certainly, he is going to be a freak when we return home. He also is considering his future:

"When I grow up I want to be an auto-rickshaw driver."

"I see."

"I want to drive people around all day. And they will pay me money."

"I see."

"I will get a really funny horn so everybody will get out of my way."

"I see."

"I want a yellow auto-rickshaw, not a gray one, with a picture of Ganesh." (Ganesh is an elephant-headed Hindu deity of good fortune. All rickshaw drivers worth their salt have Ganesh in their vehicle.)

"I see. Eat your goat curry, son."

Cole adapts well to his surroundings. He continues to speak to Dana and me as always, he speaks to his preschool teachers in their peculiar Indian brand of English, and he talks to the servants in the same Pidgin English they use with him. For example, if thirsty, he might say to Leela, “Me drinking juice, okay? Cole liking very much,” and this is perfectly understood by the intended audience. I think about correcting his English, but the truth is that he can communicate better with the servants than Dana and I can, and so, instead, I commend him for demonstrating remarkable flexibility.

On the other hand, communicating with Indian people has turned Dana into a blithering idiot. One day she comes home from work and tries to explain to Selvi and Leela that a bird pooped on her blouse.

“I am walking,” Dana cries. She marches in place in an exaggerated fashion, pumping her arms enthusiastically as if she’s in the chorus of *All That Jazz*. “Bird is coming!” She flaps her arms to simulate awkward flight. “Then, *boom*!” She throws her hands in the air. “Splat!”

“Was there a bomb?” I ask. “And why are you talking like that?”

The staff are staring at her with furrowed brow.

“We are not understanding, madam,” Selvi says.

I spin Dana around and point to the stain on her blouse. Our servants’ heads bobble as one in understanding.

✵✵✵

Dana and I have been trying without success to have a second child for some time. When our Indian doctor back home learned we were on our way to India, she suggested we take up fertility treatments there where they would be much cheaper. So, shortly after we arrive in Chennai, we begin going to a fertility clinic—accessible only by the very wealthy and quite state-of-the-art—attempting what I like to call the “turkey-baster” method of fertilization. Soon our household staff learns of this private medical matter and feels compelled to encourage our efforts.

"Madam is surely having a baby girl, saar," Selvi says, grinning. "I am not doubting it."

"Yes, saar," Dinesh agrees. "Do not give up hope, saar. We are praying very hard, saar."

CHAPTER 8: HOCUS POTUS

WHAT EVERY FOREIGN SERVICE OFFICER dreads, even more than handling a congressional delegation's wives' detail, is a presidential visit. It's March of 2000, and POTUS is coming to India. Almost the entire American staff of the consulate leaves town to prepare for Bill Clinton's visit to the city of Hyderabad in the neighboring state of Andhra Pradesh. Dana volunteers to stay in Chennai and keep the visa section running, because I have to go to Bombay on business, and we don't trust the servants alone in the house with Cole for a week.

Dana's a little bummed she won't get to meet the president, but, on the other hand, she is happy she won't have to spend a week catering to the whims of self-important, over-stressed members of the White House advance team. Ironically, while Dana is in Chennai not meeting the president, I will be staying in the same Bombay hotel as Clinton during his visit to that city. Even more strangely, the chief minister of the state of Karnataka somehow thinks I'm the president of Dell India and invites me to a reception for President Clinton to be held in the city of Bangalore a few days later. I feel like big stuff until the true head of Dell India gets wind of it at the last minute and takes away my invitation.

The night I arrive in Bombay, I encounter a rather odd situation. Normally when I travel on business I book a car and driver in advance to pick me up at the airport. This time, however, I had forgotten to do so, and I walk out of the airport at 9 p.m. without a dedicated ride. Usually, finding a taxi would be an easy proposition. A more typical challenge would be fending off the advances of a dozen or more drivers while trying to hang on to my suitcase. This night, however, is different. I stand on the sidewalk in front of the airport, and not a single person accosts me. There are no taxis, and the few people in sight are getting into private cars. There is none of the usual chaos that accompanies Indian airports. Something is definitely amiss. I head back into the airport and try to reserve a car with a prepaid taxi service.

"No taxis," yells the taxi company representative. He slams his window closed.

I go back outside and pace for a moment, wondering what to do.

"Psst, you need taxi?" A teenage Indian in sandals and torn shirt beckons. "Come. Come."

"I don't see any car," I reply.

"Taxi over there." He points to an unlit parking lot two hundred yards away.

"Forget that. I'm not crazy."

"Please don't worry. Taxi is just over there."

I'm not planning on getting mugged. "No way. Bring the taxi here."

"No, cannot."

"Sorry, I'm not interested."

The teenager shrugs, approaches a tall turbaned businessman exiting the airport and makes the same offer. The well-dressed traveler takes him up on it.

I chase them. "Excuse me! What's going on with the taxis?"

"You won't get another taxi tonight," the customer says. "They're on strike. Why don't you ride with me? We can negotiate a better deal together."

Walking the several miles into town in the dark carrying my laptop doesn't appeal to me, so I follow them and get in the back of an ancient black and yellow Ambassador. (You've never heard of this car because no one outside of India is crazy enough to buy one.) The teenager climbs in the front passenger seat, wakes up the man behind the wheel, and we are on our way.

For many miles into town there are families living in improvised shelters at the base of a wall lining the highway. These people have fixed plastic sheets in the barbed wire atop the wall and anchored the other end of the plastic with rocks on the ground, creating rustic lean-tos for protection against the elements. I watch toddlers stumbling just feet from speeding trucks, playing with the garbage that litters their only playground. I wonder what would have to happen in my life, how hopeless I would have to become, for me to leave my child to play by the highway while I try to eke out a living somewhere.

I am thinking about this when the teenager in the front of the car turns to us. He grins. "When I say, you hide backseat. OK?"

"Uh…I'm sorry. Did you say *hide?*" The teenager bobbles his head. "What's this about?" I ask my fellow passenger.

He explains that all taxis and buses in Bombay are on strike, and these gentlemen are profiting from it by picking up desperate guys like us at the airport. I'm told there will be barricades manned by striking drivers, and it would not be at all unheard of for us to be attacked. Perfect.

We stay off the main road by taking partially paved side streets on the long drive into the city, during which we are stopped two or three times by apparently drunk strikers. These men question our driver heatedly until a little money changes hands, and we are waved on. After an eternity, we arrive at my traveling companion's hotel, and, with great sadness, I say good-bye. Not only do I feel there is some safety in numbers, but he had been contrasting Sikhism with Hinduism for me, and I still have a lot of questions.

Shortly after we leave my Sikh friend behind, my companions in the front become extremely agitated.

"You must hide. Hide now!"

One hundred yards in front of us is a barricade of burning tires. A great number of men are in the street.

"Hide now!" The young man motions for me to get down on the floor.

Why did I wear a coat and tie on a travel day? I kneel on the floor and brush aside a petrified apple core.

"You need hide more now!"

The teenager climbs into the backseat and pulls from under me a blanket that has long covered the rusted-out floor of the vehicle. Cringing, I lay on my side in my heavily starched white shirt and slacks and pull my blazer over me. Through the gaping holes in the floor I could easily touch the street whizzing by just inches beneath me. The young man takes the stinking, disgusting blanket—which has obviously never been cleaned, which has likely been covering the floor of this ancient taxi for years, and onto which thousands of feet have wiped the filth of Bombay—and places it over me, taking special care to cover my head.

We roll to a stop. The men get out of the cab. I wonder if I will ever make it to my hotel. I expect any moment to be dragged from the car by an angry mob and set on fire. (Yes, this is a thing.) Through the holes in the floor I see the flickering shadows of the fire barricade. Loud talking; the car shakes; laughing; glass breaking. I'm not sure if I mentioned it, but it's easily a hundred degrees. About the moment my legs fall asleep, we begin to move. We gain some distance, and the teenager pulls off the blanket and grins over the seat at me.

"You OK, boss?"

"Awesome. Thanks."

In a quarter hour we arrive at the hotel, my person and luggage intact, where I discard my shirt and go for a late-night swim.

✹✹✹

Back at the consulate Dana is fielding calls from every Tom, Dick, and Ramachandran who wants the American president to stop by his or her house, PTA meeting, restaurant, or temple while he's in India.

"Yes sir. I'm sure President Clinton would love to attend the blessing of your new car," she says. "If you had only called us a week ago."

Then at 3 a.m.—and this is Top Secret, so I will deny I ever wrote it—the consulate notifies Dana that a supersensitive immediate night-action cable has arrived from Washington.

What can it be? Terrorists? Troop movements on the line of control? She jumps out of bed, races to the consulate, and reads the cable, only to find out that a low-level functionary in Bill's entourage will be arriving a day late and wants someone to change her hotel reservations. The bright bulb who initiated this emergency communiqué sent it to the on-duty officers of all US embassies and consulates worldwide just to make sure she got the right one. I could just hear them in Washington: "Want to see how I can wake up five hundred junior diplomats with one keystroke?"

While on duty this week, Dana also is in charge of American Citizen Services. This is the department in an American embassy or consulate that assists Americans who get in trouble abroad, among other things. (Before you ask, American diplomats can't get you out of jail if you commit a crime abroad. Foreign jails are full of hapless

Americans who "can't believe this happened to me.") She takes a call about a head-on collision in a remote area involving an American mother and daughter. Mom is badly injured and rushed to surgery at a local hospital. The daughter talks with Dana for an hour in the middle of the night about the squalid conditions in the hospital, the fresh blood on the floors, and the doctors' refusal to give her any information about her mother.

In a separate incident, an elderly American dies in a hotel room while vacationing alone. Dana makes arrangements to have his body returned home, but at his family's request, all his belongings are to be given away. Narayanan, our gardener, gets a brand-new pair of Nikes, the first pair of closed-toe shoes he has ever owned. The rest we leave in front of the house for the neighborhood to pick through. Needless to say, nothing is wasted.

CHAPTER 9: LIFESTYLES OF THE SOMEWHAT RICH AND
FAMOUS

W E'VE BEEN IN CHENNAI FOUR months or so, and, with my
near-death experience in a Bombay taxi, the live worms in
our water—we distill it, worms and all—and running the daily
gauntlet of life in a developing country, in general, we are beginning
to tire of exotic. In fact, it's getting kind of irritating. (Our sponsor,
Nancy, tells us we are now in the "realization" stage of our
relationship with India.) Still, we manage to entertain ourselves with
unique opportunities that our diplomatic status and newly found
relative wealth afford us.

Dana receives an engraved invitation to a dinner show
benefiting a traditional crafts foundation. We and Chennai's Indian
elite are serenaded for a night by South Indian pop superstar
Anuradha Sriram. She brings the house down singing
extemporaneous folk music, as well as hits from her *Chennai Girl*
album. (I got this partial translation of one of her songs from a dicey
Indian website with an average of ten pop-up ads per second: "Are
you the moon that shone in the college in the sky? That grazed all
juvenility of the students' hearts? O, haiku! O, haiku! I love you."
Not sure what any of that means, but it sounds pretty cool in Tamil.)
Our Indian friends, green with envy, later tell us this is the Indian
equivalent of enjoying a private performance by Taylor Swift.

At the end of the performance there is a benefit auction; top prize is a trip to anywhere in Europe on the German airline Lufthansa. Bidding opens, and no one raises a hand. We wait.

"It looks like the elite are a little stingy tonight," I whisper to Dana.

Time passes. No bids.

"Gosh, is anyone going to even bid on this? How embarrassing."

Nothing.

Then, for some reason known but to God, I raise my hand. I'll just get things started; surely someone will overbid me.

"Sold! To Mr. Buford for sixty-five thousand rupees!"

Okay. Calm down. It's no big deal. Sixty-five thousand rupees sounds pretty good for business-class tickets to Europe. I can take the family to Rome or Paris. We could use a trip.

"Here is your *ticket*, Mr. Buford," the exuberant emcee cries.

"Excuse me, did you say *ticket*? That's not 'tickets'?"

"Congratulations! You purchased one ticket, business-class, to anywhere in Europe."

I look at Dana. Her face is red. Hmm...let's see...one ticket for sixty-five thousand rupees...that's about...two thousand bucks. I almost throw up on Anuradha Sriram's mother sitting next to me. This is the Indian equivalent of almost throwing up on Taylor Swift's mother.

Due to my selfless patronage of traditional arts, Dana and I are invited to dine at Anuradha Sriram's table that night, but I don't enjoy it a bit. I recall the time my Great Aunt Birdie caught me looking at my dad's secret stash of *Playboys*.

"Boy, you just wait until your father gets home," she hissed, snatching the magazines away. "He's going to wear your hide out!"

I cowered in my room the rest of the day until Dad came home and told me to cry out in pain as he slapped his belt on the wall. I was very confused by this, but it satisfied Aunt Birdie. Not sure if Dad got a spanking. Anyway, I'm sitting across the table from Dana knowing I got it coming, feeling like I'm six again and waiting for Dad to come home.

"You just *had* to start the bidding, didn't you?" Dana asks again and again on the long ride home. "What are we going to do with one ticket?"

"Well, you were the one who made us go to the stupid benefit in the first place," I counter. "You know I have a problem with auctions."

"We've never even been to an auction, butthead."

"Oh, see, now, that's not nice. We'll go to Rome, and you'll thank me. I forgive you in advance." I stick out my tongue at her.

The mention of Rome cheers her a bit, but I keep secret my prediction that Dana and Cole are not going to like sitting in coach without me, which is where they will be because I'm not about to shell out another four thousand bucks so all of us can ride biz class together. My prediction proves correct.

"The ticket, you see, is nontransferable," I explain to Dana, "and since it has my name on it, you see, and we can't all afford to ride biz class—"

"I'll have to ride in coach with Cole."

"Uh…yeah, that's about the size of it." I give her my saddest puppy dog eyes, to no visible effect.

"Jerk."

As it turns out, the cheapest ticket from Chennai to Rome is on Air Lanka and requires an overnight stay in a grubby airport departure lounge in the Sri Lankan capital, Colombo. To this day Dana still believes what I said about my business-class ticket being nontransferable, and I'm not saying a word. Serves her right for giving me so much grief about accidentally buying that ticket, don't you think?

So that is how we get to have dinner with the most popular star in India, who, incidentally, eats like a horse. And I appreciate a woman who can eat. In college I dated thin, little things that would just sit across the table watching me stuff my face. And, as often as not, *I* would get stuck with the bill for what *they* didn't eat.

"Why aren't you eating?" I'd ask.

"I already ate," or "I'm not hungry," would be the reply, forcing me to wonder why we were at a restaurant at all.

On the other hand, my wife, like Anuradha Sriram, can really put it away, and this fact led to our marriage. On our first date we wound up at a crowded party and unable to talk over the noise. I lamely asked Dana if she'd like to go back to my place for some homemade pecan pie. (Gentlemen, try this approach. I can personally guarantee she won't have heard it before. Important: You have to find a pecan pie!) Dana, unable to resist any dessert, readily accepted, and she ended up taking home with her what she didn't eat right away—although she ate most of it right away. To this day, it's best to keep your hands and feet away from her mouth when she's eating.

Even as a junior American diplomat, you're a big fish in the small pond of the Chennai social scene. Our next post turns out to be at a very large embassy, and Dana sits so low on the totem pole that we don't get invited to a single diplomatic function the entire two years we are there. But in Chennai, any American diplomat is something of a big deal—we have VIP parking spots reserved for us at the mall—and so we get invited to dine with Nawab Mohammed Abdul Ali, aka the Prince of Arcot, at his favorite restaurant, along with several other Americans from the consulate.

The prince arrives late with a five-member entourage—a fashion designer, a real estate magnate, a "professional intellectual," and two other well-to-do Indians—and the American consul general opens with some innocuous small talk. True to their training, each of the other diplomats at the table manages to interject, at an appropriate lull, an insightful question or comment demonstrating his or her knowledge of and interest in the prince and India. The prince, however, remains uncommunicative, responding in short sentences or a simple "yes" or "no," which leaves the diplomats in the room scrambling to fill the void left by the prince's abrupt trailings-off.

Eventually, the deafening sound of the wheels grinding in the junior officers' heads becomes too much for me to bear. So, after listening to this banter for an hour and figuring that all of the "young dips" have scored enough points with the consul general, I begin with the question I have been waiting to ask since we got the invitation to dine with His Highness.

"So, Prince, I thought the Indian royals lost their titles at independence fifty years ago. How did you manage to hang on to yours?"

The American consul general chokes on his wine. There is a long moment of silence. The prince clears his throat and recounts his family history in detail, beginning with the second caliph of Islam in 580 AD, moving on to an ancestor's leading the Muslim invasion of India in the sixteenth century, and culminating with an uncle making a hell of a deal allowing him to keep his royal title after independence. I find the story fascinating, but by the time the prince finishes, I think I'm the only one at the table still awake. I decide not to hit him with my follow-up question: "So what exactly does a prince do, anyway?" At the end of the evening, I invite the prince and his wife to dinner at our palace, but they never come.

Harish is quickly becoming a permanent fixture of our lives in India. He drops by for tea and a chat, and he always has a friend he wants us to meet. The consulate Americans are divided on Harish. Some avoid him, assuming he is a cynical visa-seeker; others consider him a great friend. We're honestly starting to like him. He introduces us to the Chennai soirée circuit, and soon we begin to receive from friends of friends invitations to some event almost every weekend. Many of these parties are given by the stodgy old money of Chennai, a small and incestuous group into which we are invited as token foreigners to spend evenings listening to them brag about which American or British private universities their sons and daughters are attending.

Maybe I'm being too harsh. We find these parties interesting from an anthropological standpoint, and we do make some good friends at these events whose company we truly enjoy. Yet many of these people are the same pretentious bores who populate well-heeled parties anywhere. Dana and I are invited because Dana is an American diplomat, and I'm sure many of the elite at these parties wouldn't have given us the time of day if they had known I had once been a garbage collector.

We find that our American Consulate friends are not on the Indian socialites' guest list. After all, most of them find the idea of listening to an Oxford-educated Indian poet pontificate about the decadence of the West entirely insufferable. We do too, but we like the food, and since Chennai offers little other nightlife besides parties given by the foreigners-only crowd, we just laugh and head back to the food. The food—again, extremely important to Dana—consists of outlandish spreads of delightful Indian delicacies catered by all the correct restaurants, and so we discreetly pig out. We also love seeing the fancy houses. Entirely lost on us is the presence of certain famous Indians: movie stars, sports celebs, politicians.

If Dinesh drives us to these affairs, he might say, "Did you talk with Shah Rukh Khan? He's a famous movie star," or "That woman you bumped into on the way out—she's the president's daughter." We take pains to remember that all this pomp and circumstance is just make-believe, and after a while we find some genuine friends, like Rochelle.

Rochelle is a fascinating soft-spoken woman in her sixties who lives just a few blocks from us and who begins to include us at her parties and sponsored events. She is down-to-earth and kind, and one day she tells me she belongs to a small community of South Indian Jews.

I had assumed she was Hindu. "I didn't even know there were South Indian Jews," I tell her.

Rochelle finds my ignorance delightful and happily tells me the history of her people. Jews are believed to have arrived in South India as early as the sixth century BC. Tradition has it they were fleeing the invading armies of Nebuchadnezzar, a man not exactly famous for religious tolerance. These Jews found sanctuary in India until about two thousand years later, when they were persecuted by the colonizing Portuguese and many of their synagogues were burned. They eventually rebuilt, but many of their number immigrated to Israel. Where Jews remain in India, their communities are in danger of disappearing altogether, without enough males of age to perform traditional rites in the synagogues.

We visit one of these small synagogues in Kochi on India's Malabar Coast. Originally constructed in the sixteenth century, the building had been destroyed by the Portuguese and later rebuilt. Near the synagogue is a small enclave of shops with Jewish names on them that appears out of place, surrounded by India on all sides.

CHAPTER 10: WE ARE FAMILY

SELVI, OUR ORIGINAL HOUSEKEEPER, WHO has been with us since our first night in India, for whom was invented the adage "if you want something done right, you have to do it yourself," leaves us to take a job closer to home. I can find a dozen good reasons to fire her on an average day, but when she tells me the news, I'm genuinely sad to see her go. Who is going to make me laugh? It certainly isn't for her competence that we've kept her around. I think it's something about her profound laziness that appeals to me at the most basic level.

Not surprisingly, Selvi offers to help me find her replacement, and her older sister, Shanthi, instantly appears in the kitchen. I'm optimistic that Shanthi will work harder, if only because she has been out of work for months and clearly needs a job. So a few days later, Shanthi, her two kids, and her husband, Dom, an auto-rickshaw driver, move all their worldly belongings into the unoccupied servants' quarters in our backyard. Everything they own, except for two mammoth cooking pots and a single-burner kerosene stove, fits in one dilapidated suitcase—for a family of four. There are no toys, no TV, no refrigerator, no Xbox. We have more stuff left unpacked on the top shelf of our closet. To describe the lot as "hardscrabble" would be a gross understatement. I am happy to offer Shanthi employment and a rent-free abode for her family.

Selvi gathers her things, bids farewell to Cole, and leaves, crying, out the back door. Then she stops and beckons me to her side.

"Master," she whispers, "one thing I must tell you now."

Uh-oh. What now? "Yes, Selvi. What is it? And don't call me 'master.'"

"That cook, Leela—"

"Yes, Selvi. What is it?"

"Please be careful, saar. Please take care the child."

"What do you mean, Selvi?"

"Leela is witch, saar. Everybody knows it. All servants knows it."

I laugh out loud.

"It's true, saar! Please take careful."

"I will, Selvi. Thank you."

Fabulous. As if I didn't have enough to deal with, now our cook is a witch. After some thought, however, I conclude that if Leela really were a witch she sure as heck wouldn't be cooking for me.

I only find out months later from Shanthi the real reason for Selvi's departure. It seems that rumors abounded in the servant community that Selvi and I were having an affair! Even if Selvi and I had even been remotely attracted to each other, it would have been exceedingly difficult for us to carry on a clandestine love affair with five other servants and a three-year-old in the house, not to mention the daily maintenance calls and visits of door-to-door rug sellers, knife sharpeners, snake charmers, etc. Anyway, her husband got wind of the rumors, and Selvi had to quit.

To hear her tell it, my new housekeeper, Shanthi, epitomizes the oppressed and long-suffering Indian woman. Born to a family of several girls in a country that places a relatively low value on females, she married at a young age, survived an alcoholic and abusive husband, and had a daughter, Priya, an unfortunate event her husband blamed on her. Her husband then killed himself. It was her second husband, however, that Shanthi says was a real bastard. When she became pregnant, he beat her and forced her to drink cleaning fluid in hopes of inducing a spontaneous abortion. He died in an accident shortly before she gave birth to a boy, Mani. When she comes to work for me, Shanthi is with her third man, Dom, who by all accounts—including Shanthi's—is a deadbeat. Cole is tickled pink because Dom gives him free rides around the yard in his autorickshaw.

"But he is no drinking and he is not beating me, saar," Shanthi says in Dom's defense, and that is good enough for her. With Mani eight and Priya thirteen, I entertain a curious notion that our children can transcend barriers of culture, income, class, and language and play together happily. Boy, am I wrong.

Shortly after they move in, we invite Shanthi's kids to participate in our backyard Easter egg hunt. Since they live in our backyard, it seems ridiculous not to ask them to take part. Of course, they have no idea what to do, but after seeing us hide candy-filled eggs, they quickly figure it out. Unfortunately, Priya and Mani follow Cole around, fawning over him as if he is the crown prince. (And, for all practical purposes, he may as well be.) Shanthi at first won't let her children keep any of the candy. Mani and Priya duly turn over their loot to Cole until I insist they be allowed to keep it. Basically, the whole thing is an unmitigated disaster.

When the children play games in the yard and Cole finds himself losing, the rules are changed to ensure his success. If Cole behaves selfishly or rudely, Mani and Priya apologize profusely and immediately give him whatever will pacify him, encouraged in this practice by their parents. I explain several times to Shanthi and Dom that Cole is not allowed to be rude and that Mani and Priya are not Cole's servants, but it just doesn't compute. Shanthi simply looks at me as if I'm from some far-off planet and continues as before.

One day, I walk outside to find Dom slapping and shouting at Priya because Cole has thrown a fit after losing a round of hide-and-seek. I had only that day made a speech about how Mani and Priya should treat Cole as they would any child at school. I realize that just isn't going to happen, and for me to ask it is naïve and unfair. This means that I will have to limit their play together. Trying to do that, however, proves almost impossible, and I'm relieved when Shanthi & Co. move out of the servants' quarters before too long.

Now we have nine people directly or indirectly dependent upon our household, and things begin to spiral out of control. My job requires me to travel more and more, and although I know we have too many people around, the easiest thing is to do nothing. Mani innocently suggests I have someone train the staff to perform traditional dance just to give them all something to do. That idea isn't met with enthusiasm by the adults. Only Dinesh really works very hard (except for Dana and me), but I'm too busy and too soft to fire someone. Dinesh becomes indispensable to us, managing things in our absence and leading the others by example.

Meanwhile, things aren't going well at work. My job is to assist an Indian sales team that reports to the head of Dell India in Bangalore (home of KFC). My boss, however, is at the Dell Asia corporate headquarters in Singapore. I only met him once for about five minutes when business coincidentally took us to Malaysia at the same time. The head of Dell India and my boss in Singapore have very different ideas about what my job is supposed to be, *and* they hate each other's guts. So every time I fly to Bangalore, I'm asked by Dell India to do one thing, and then my boss calls from Singapore and tells me to do something else. I'm trying the best I can to make them both happy and am not succeeding.

CHAPTER 11: BISCUITS AND CRAZY

IN SUMMER I GO TO Australia for a Dell event, and normally I would be thrilled. However, I'm feeling daily more apprehensive about the nanny, Heather, and the idea of leaving Cole in her hands for a week dampens my excitement. There's nothing I can put a finger on, but something just doesn't feel right. Heather does a good job when I'm around, but I know she and our cook, Leela, don't like each other. I wonder if their antipathy toward each other will affect Cole. Dana promises me she will come home from work as soon as possible every day during my absence. Dinesh, watching me in the rearview mirror on the way to the airport, speaks up to reassure me even though I haven't shared my concern with him.

"I'll taking care of Cole, saar. Not to worry."

I already know enough about Dinesh to trust him, and, in the end, he turns out to be our best babysitter of all.

The Australia trip will be good for me because my boss is flying in from Singapore for the event, and he assures me I'll finally get some face time. Feuding between my boss and the chief of Dell India over my duties and responsibilities has reached the level of open warfare. The head of Dell India tells me he doesn't care what Dell's Singapore HQ says; I need to support him or there will be no Dell India to support. My boss in Singapore tells me to hold out; the Dell India chief's days are numbered. I'm still stuck in the middle.

Despite his promises, when I get to Australia my boss won't meet me to discuss the issue.

"Just ten minutes, Jerry. Things are getting out of hand."

"Yeah, sure. I got to run off to a meeting now, but I'll catch up with you later."

He never does, and nothing changes.

I arrive home from my weeklong trip to find my own little human resources crisis: Leela the cook and Shanthi the new housekeeper are in the front yard shouting at each other as little Narayanan stands between them brandishing his broom like a sword. Cole sits on the sidelines with furrowed brow, while Heather eggs them on.

I climb out of the jeep. "All right, the party's over."

"This is not a party," Cole cries indignantly, and everybody laughs.

I question Leela, and she quickly seals her fate. She insists (again) that I look favorably upon her, a devout Christian, and shun the servants who are "dirty Hindus."

"They are jealous because I am Christian. This is why they hate me." (This fails to explain why she can't get along with Heather, who is also Christian.)

"Leela is not a nice person to us," Dinesh reveals to me in private.

I figured others in the house receive the same kind of grumbling complaints I get from Leela, but I was not aware of the severity of the problem. It's obvious I have to let her go. I simply can't be away on business with a potentially explosive situation at home. Dana agrees, but only if I'll do the dirty work.

I find Leela in the kitchen. "Leela, I'm sorry, but you need to find a job with another family."

"I don't understand, sir."

"You can't work here anymore."

Leela drops to her knees. She hugs my legs. "Oh, my Lord Jesus, help me!"

"Leela, that's enough. I'll pay you for the entire month."

"Please, sir. Please!" she pleads. Tears are streaming down her face. "No, it cannot be true."

"I'm afraid it's true."

She touches her forehead to my feet.

"Leela, stop it."

Leela clutches her chest. "Oh...oh...my heart!" She rolls on her side. "I am having heart attack!" She rolls the other way. "Aieeeee! The pain! I am dying surely."

"Well, I'm happy to call you a doctor, but you still can't work here. Please get up."

I look up and catch Shanthi, Narayanan, and Heather watching the scene through the kitchen window. I give them a dirty look, and they quickly turn away.

"Satan controls you, sir," Leela cries. "He is speaking these words to punish me."

"Nope, I'm afraid not. It's just me, and I've warned you several times."

Leela lets me help her to her feet and then snatches her hand away.

"Out, Devil! Out, Satan!"

As Leela prepares to exorcise me, I tell her to get her things and hit the road. I leave to check on Cole. When I return, Leela is frantically stuffing her purse with kitchen utensils. For the next few days Leela returns to cry on my feet and exhort Satan to leave me.

"Sir, God will surely punish you," she sobs.

"Pray for me," I say and close the gate in her face.

Shanthi looks terrified.

"I certainly hope she's not a witch," I tell her. "Because if she is, I'm in big trouble."

Shanthi bobbles her head, dead serious.

Leela calls us periodically for months, moaning that her husband is too old to work and that she is in desperate straits. I feel bad for her and once almost try to get her a job with a friend until Dana reminds me why we fired her and that she's a thief. It's too bad she couldn't get along with those "dirty Hindus," because she was a good cook.

After I give Leela the boot, I realize how spoiled I've gotten after just a few months with a cook. I've barely lifted a finger in the kitchen since we arrived in India, and to suddenly find myself there again puts me in a rotten mood. I should also explain that in Chennai you don't just roll up to the store and get a week's worth of groceries in one fell swoop. Shopping involves navigating the crowded vegetable market and haggling over the price of vegetables—difficult when you don't speak the language—and, if you can stomach the flies, braving the meat market, and then traipsing across town to the expensive specialty store for any foreign ingredients, and so on. Or, like foreigners and well-to-do Indians, you hire someone to do this hot and time-consuming work for you.

A couple of days after Leela's departure Shanthi interrupts me in the kitchen while I'm trying to figure out what to make for dinner. I'm not in the best of spirits, and I have a sinking feeling she's going to ask me for a loan.

"Master?"

"Don't call me 'master.'"

"Saar?"

"What do you need, Shanthi?" I busily continue searching for something to assemble for supper.

"Saar. I am cook more than ten years." I am slowly gaining interest. "I can cook North Indian, South Indian, Chinese, American, and Japanese."

I freeze. "You can cook Japanese food?"

"I work for Japanese family six years. She teaching me everything."

"Can you read recipes?"

"Yes, I read. I also make fried cheese."

"Fried cheese?" I want to kiss her. "Show me what you can do."

To our pleasant surprise we eat very well that night.

"Why didn't you tell me you knew how to cook?"

Shanthi smiles and says, "I know you fire Leela sooner or later. I just wait. This very easier."

Desperate for Tex-Mex, I undertake to teach Shanthi how to make fajitas with all the trimmings. We're luckier than most foreigners, because a Muslim butcher from Bangalore supplies the commissary of the American Consulate with cheap, high-quality beef, something not readily available in India, where the cow is sacred to the Hindu majority. I teach Shanthi how to marinate, grill, and serve the steak, and make *pico de gallo* and guacamole, which, to my amusement, she persists in calling "avocado chutney." She learns to make fresh flour tortillas and dubs these "Mexican *chapatti*." A chapatti is, well, an Indian tortilla. Although Shanthi makes many great non-Indian dishes, she is endearingly unaware of our ideas about what should be served with what. For example, when I'm not watching she could serve lasagna with Southern-style biscuits and cream gravy. Or she might serve vegetable sushi with chicken-fried steak.

As I mentioned, the cow is sacred to Hindus, which means that cows roam the streets with impunity, creating great traffic jams when they decide to rest in the middle of a major intersection. Hinduism is a religion that respects all life, no matter how lowly it might seem, but the cow is king, and Hindus treat these animals with the greatest respect. There are even nursing homes for older cows, and for a Hindu to harm a cow is a big no-no.

In South India, Hindus not only don't eat beef but many also refrain from eating dead animal of any type. At the very least, they might become vegetarian before a visit to an important temple. Once a year our driver, Dinesh, stops shaving and abstains from all meat for a month before a pilgrimage to his favorite temple. Additionally, many high-caste Hindus place restrictions on themselves regarding the preparation of their food. For example, a member of the Brahmin caste will, traditionally, eat food prepared only by a fellow Brahmin. To not do so invites impurity of the soul. A good Brahmin friend who has come to our house many times politely refuses so much as a drink of water. He has declined a dozen invitations to dinner and always suggests we go to a favorite restaurant when pressed.

Adherents to Jainism, one of India's most ancient religions, are so serious about not harming another creature that some of them cover their mouths with cloth so they don't accidentally inhale an insect. Not only will Jains not eat any animal, many also will not eat root vegetables, as some living creature might have been harmed during their harvest. Of course, India's minority Muslim population, for their part, won't eat pork. By comparison, we Christians are hedonistic omnivores.

You can imagine, what with all this pious abstention on the part of our Indian friends, throwing a party can be tricky. A good host carefully labels each item so as to avoid any embarrassment. We decide the easiest way to please the most people is to simply serve all-veg food at parties. This might still exclude some Jains and the pickier Brahmins, but we figure folks with such strict dietary taboos are used to going hungry when they go out.

Interestingly, some Indians don't apply these restrictions at all when traveling overseas. Gone are the days when rich Hindus carried their own water on trips abroad so as to remain ritually "clean." The matriarch of a Jain family once proudly proclaimed to us: "Never has so much as one egg crossed our threshold." When traveling in the US, however, she admits the entire family pigs out on all the steak they can get their hands on. Upon returning to India, they shed any leather or other animal products they've picked up abroad and return to a life of strict religious observance.

CHAPTER 12: BARRAGE MAHAL

MY MOTHER, FATHER, AND NIECE, Tiffany, arrive for a monthlong visit. My mom almost dies of boredom en route; when they change planes in London, they aren't even halfway. Once in Chennai, my family amuses themselves buying a year's worth of supplies of their favorite prescription drugs for one-twentieth of the price back home. I take Tiffany to northern India to see the Taj Mahal, which is definitely worth the trip. My mother is too tired: "If you've seen one four-hundred-year-old wonder of the world, you've seen them all." And my father won't do anything without my mother. Tiffany, who is fourteen at the time, has the experience of a lifetime.

Tiffany and I fly from Chennai to Delhi and head to New Delhi Railway Station in hopes of buying tickets to Agra, the city lucky enough to claim the Taj Mahal. I'd been warned of a station overcrowded with travelers, touts, homeless beggars, and con artists—a lot like New York's Port Authority bus terminal—not the kind of place where you want to be a foreign tourist. My guidebook reads, "No one knows for sure how many people in and around the station make their living scamming tourists, but it's more than a few." In fact, the fun starts in the taxi on our way to the station.

"Saar, you want tickets to Agra?" our driver asks, grinning broadly, not watching the road at all.

I cringe at his dental work. "No thanks."

He ignores my answer. "I can sell you tickets at discount price."

"That's kind of you, but we'll buy our tickets in the station."

"The train station is closed now. You can only buy tickets from taxi driver for early morning train."

"Oh, then that's OK. We are taking the night train."

"Same thing for late night train."

"Sorry, I mean we'll take the afternoon train."

"Morning, noon, or nighttime. My tickets much cheaper."

"Take us to the station now, or we're getting out of the car."

When we get to the station, beggars mob us. Two paraplegic men on makeshift four-wheel dollies chase us through the traffic, navigating with their arms. The destitute elderly shove their empty bowls at us. It is not yet 7 a.m. We make a run for the building and cower in a corner.

Tiffany is crying. "I want to go home!"

I put an arm around her. "Everything's going to be OK," I say, but I'm not so sure and I want to go home too.

A young Indian man loitering in the shadows makes a beeline for us. "Excuse me, can you tell me how to get to Connaught Circle?"

I am wary. "Listen, my friend. We are surrounded by at least a thousand Indian people, but you ask a couple of American tourists for directions?"

He walks away, dejected. Clearly, my "honeymoon" phase with India is over.

Tiffany is embarrassed. "Chill out, Uncle Greg."

OK. Chill.

With something like, "I don't care if the building catches on fire, don't let our bags out of your sight," I leave Tiffany to sit on our luggage while I go for tickets. Oddly, all the ticket windows are closed, and this is a bad thing because the train to Agra leaves in thirty minutes. I run upstairs where I had read a ticket window exists exclusively for foreign tourists. It's closed too. Half a dozen or so men loiter in front. As soon as they see me, they snap from their reverie and race to be of service to a needy tourist. Imagine my surprise that one of them is the young man looking for Connaught Circle. He catches up to me as I flee down the stairs.

"Saar, I know where you can buy a train ticket for Agra."

"You do? I thought you were looking for Connaught Circle."

He smiles. "Saar, I work for the Tourist Information Center for Indian Railways."

"Really? Nice to meet you. I'm the president of the United States."

"Saar, my office is very near."

"Hang on a sec." I whip out my *Lonely Planet* and find the page where it describes the exact scam this guy is pulling.

"Let's see. According to this, you meet me upstairs where the ticket window is closed. You tell me you work for the Tourist Information Center. According to my book, your office must be one of those four or five offices just over there with "Tourist Information Center" above the door, right? When I get over there, you're going to tell me the only way I can get a ticket for this morning's train is to buy one from you, plus a small commission. Right?"

"Saar, you just come look."

I push my way through the crowd of beggars surrounding Tiffany. "Come on. Maybe this is legit."

We walk across the street to an office. Three men jump out of their chairs as we enter. They offer drinks, and I take care that they are opened in front of us. These men spend five minutes or so bullshitting us before I cut them off.

"How much?"

They continue with the crap.

"Look, I just want two round-trip tickets to Agra. If you can sell them to me at a decent price, I might buy. I don't mind paying a commission. Just tell me what the catch is."

"Saar, there is no commission," one of them assures me. His companions bobble their heads in unison.

"And the tickets are free too, I guess. Well, thank you. We'd like two second class, round trip."

Two slips of paper that look as if they might be train tickets are coaxed from an ancient dot-matrix printer so loud Tiffany covers her ears.

"The cost for each ticket is 2,851 rupees."

"Wow! That sounds like an awful lot because, you see, my guidebook says the fare should be about forty-nine rupees."

"Prices have gone up, saar. That book is old."

I point at a solar calculator on a desk. "Can I borrow that?" Connaught Circle Man glumly hands it to me. "Let's see," I say, running the numbers, "that's a 5,810 percent increase since this book was published seven months ago. Well, I guess we can't afford to go now. But thanks for the drinks!"

With this, we hastily leave. When we get back in the station, the official ticket window has opened, and we buy tickets to Agra for fifty-five rupees.

The city of Agra apparently hasn't had a face-lift since the completion of its most famous building in 1653. I mean, the place is seriously rough around the edges. As we inch into town on the train from Delhi, for several minutes we can't look in any direction without seeing someone defecating on the ground.

"Gross," Tiffany cries. "Gross, gross, gross."

"Don't judge," I admonish. "No one *wants* to do their business in the public eye."

Public toilets for the masses in India can be few and far between, and only the well-to-do have plumbing in their homes. When public toilets are available, you're often better off just going on the side of the road like everyone else. (Trust me on this one. I still have nightmares.) By the way, if you're a pampered Westerner, you'd better carry your own toilet paper with you unless you don't leave the hotel. Like many peoples in the world, Indians use their left hand and a splash of water (if available) to complete the same job we accomplish with toilet paper. And, in case you were wondering, this is why Indians don't eat with their left hand.

As we disembark in Agra, a swarm of hopeful hawkers, ready to part with anything under the sun for the "best price," jogs toward us. Porters reach for our luggage. Beggars stretch out their hands. Tiffany is withering under this barrage. She is mobbed by at least a dozen men selling Taj Mahal miniatures and begins to cry.

❉ ❉ ❉

In 1525, a guy named Babur—a Muslim descendant of both brutal conquerors Genghis Khan and Tamerlane—invaded predominantly Hindu India and founded the Mughal Dynasty, ushering in a golden age of architecture, arts, and literature. Many of the most famous structures in India today were commissioned by the Mughals, including the world-famous building we have come to see.

About four hundred years ago, Mumtaz Mahal, the second wife of the fifth Mughal emperor, Shah Jahan, died in childbirth. Heartbroken, Shah Jahan commissioned in her honor the world's most extravagant monument ever built in the name of love, the mausoleum known as the Taj Mahal. It took twenty-two years, a butt-load of money, and the lives of many workers from India and

Central Asia to complete the structure, and centuries later it remains the unofficial emblem of Indian tourism. The timeless beauty of the Taj Mahal seen from afar is surpassed only by the exquisite detail apparent when viewing it at arm's length. Its white marble walls inscribed with extensive passages from the Koran and inlaid with thousands of semiprecious stones, the Taj Mahal is a must-see on any visit to India.

Legend and some archaeological evidence exists to indicate Shah Jahan planned to build an exact replica of the Taj Mahal in black marble to serve as his own tomb on the opposite side of the Yamuna River. Whether prompted by the outrageous expense of the project or simply impatient to rule, Shah Jahan's son Aurangzeb deposed his father and imprisoned him in the Octagonal Tower of Agra Fort, also built by Shah Jahan. No saint himself, incidentally, Shah Jahan was only able secure his own place as emperor by having all his male relatives put to death. At any rate, Shah Jahan spent the last seven years of his life imprisoned in Agra Fort, from where he couldn't help but behold an absolutely stunning view of his most memorable accomplishment, the Taj Mahal. How's that for poetic irony? Tiffany and I stand in the Octagonal Tower and muse upon the fate of good ol' Shah Jahan, mesmerized, as he surely had been, by the beauty of the sun setting on his wife's mausoleum.

We return to Agra Station for a train back to Delhi, from where we'll fly back to Chennai. We're alarmed to hear a rumor that the train to Delhi leaves in ten minutes, and we realize that if we don't get on that train we'll miss our flight to Chennai. This train remains only a rumor because there is neither a posted schedule nor anyone who seems to know for sure. A rusted sign marks the tourist information booth, but it's clearly been closed since before I was born. We read of a separate ticket window for foreign tourists, but apparently it doesn't exist.

There are several hundred people in line—I use the term "line" loosely—shoving one another about in front of a bank of windows with tiny openings at the bottom. Behind the windows sit several carefree men laughing, chatting, and doing just about anything but selling train tickets. In fact, between the lot of them they can only spare one person to work, leaving the other half-dozen windows closed. Desperate men—there are no women—fight for the privilege of shoving their money through the tiny slot in the window and shouting their destination. The station employee sells tickets at a snail's pace and turns frequently to sip tea and laugh at his colleagues' jokes. I realize we have no chance of fighting our way to the window. I'm despondent and trying to figure out where we can spend the night.

"I'm not missing that train," Tiffany cries.

With a roar, she dives into the fray and shoves herself halfway to the window until she can go no further. She bursts into tears, screaming to all who listen that she is about to miss her train and be lost forever and die right there in front of everybody if she doesn't get two tickets for the next train to Delhi.

More out of surprise than pity, I think, at seeing this foreign teenager melt down in their midst, the men shove her forward to the window. Her money is taken, two tickets appear, and we make a run for the trains.

"What just happened?" I ask.

Tiffany wipes the tears from her face. "Piece of cake!"

The tickets don't indicate a train number, platform, departure time, seat number, or destination, but somehow we get on the right train and make it home.

CHAPTER 13: FOOLS BARGAIN

W E LOVE HAVING VISITORS FROM home, because we get to experience vicariously the shock, joy, and wonder that outsiders naturally feel upon their first visit to India. As impossible as it sounds, we are already becoming accustomed to the daily craziness that is India, and our guests' reactions remind us how remarkable it all is. In essence, our life in Chennai has become almost *routine*, and when guests show up, it feels as if I'm watching myself get off the plane again.

Our friends Carolyn and Lisa grace our home in the month of August. Leaving Dana hard at work at the consulate, Dinesh and I escort these two on great shopping forays across South India.

"They shop more than any people I have ever met," Dinesh whispers as we struggle to remain awake while they browse.

"Yeah, well, at least *you're* getting paid to be here."

One day we go to Kanchipuram, reportedly *the* place to find silk in South India. Outside of chain stores with set prices, bargaining is done almost anywhere in India. Indeed, it is expected, and, by the time Carolyn and Lisa arrive, it has become something of a sport for me: the feints, the brinkmanship, and the satisfaction of arriving at a mutually beneficial deal.

Carolyn insists I drive the hardest of bargains on her behalf, but Lisa asks, "Why do we even bother? It's so cheap."

Over the past several months I've struggled with this question, and so I tell her my position: There's nothing charitable about paying a ridiculous price for something. Allowing yourself to be taken for a sucker can even breed contempt. Whether you agree with that or not, as an Indian friend told me, "If a vendor's not going to make any money off a deal, she's not going to make the deal." But bargaining's a funny thing; newbies, including me, walk away from things they really want because pride gets in the way. We don't feel like the other side gives enough, and so we walk away irritated and empty-handed.

And, ladies, in case you didn't know it, men are prideful beasts. You should *not* let them do your bargaining. They will walk away from the only thing you've ever wanted, which to them looks silly, because the young man in the market wouldn't split the difference on the last five *centavos*. And then you'll just end up buying the same thing at another stall for more or, worse, go home empty-handed. Best thing is to focus on what you're willing to pay for something rather than how many times you can get the vendor to come down. If something's really special to you, who cares if someone else paid a little less for the same thing or if you "won"?

Well aware of the pitfalls of bargaining with someone else's money, I refuse Carolyn's request. "No way! No way I'm doing your bargaining."

Carolyn takes my hand, pouting. "But I thought you were my friend…"

I snatch my hand away. "Exactly why I don't want to do your bargaining."

In the end, of course, I relent. "Okay, but only if you promise you won't hate me."

"I promise!"

"And you won't butt in."

"Never!"

Each shop—most are mere huts rather than bricks and mortar—slips Dinesh a commission of forty or fifty rupees under the table for bringing us in. Dinesh is tickled pink and gives us the running total of his earnings so we can giggle along with him. On our fifth stop several people with rupee signs in their eyes greet us with ice-cold soft drinks. We are ushered into the inner sanctum, where a man sits cross-legged on the floor.

"Welcome to the home of the best fabrics in Kanchipuram! I am Amit."

"Thank you, but we're not here to buy," I say. "Sorry to waste your time." Lisa and Carolyn eye me with suspicion.

Amit's head bobbles. "Please, sit." Chairs are brought in. "From what country do you come?"

"Oh, we're locals down from Chennai."

He frowns. "I see." Brightening again, he adds, "Would your ladies like to see our fabrics?"

I look at Carolyn on my left. I look at Lisa on my right. "No. I don't think so."

Amit nods, and two young women lay beautiful silk pieces on the rug before us. Carolyn and Lisa are impressed. They select several items and whisper to me which ones they're not prepared to leave without. I put these items in a pile.

"How much are you asking?"

"Ah, you have chosen the very best." After much feigned contemplation Amit says, "Twenty thousand rupees is the least I can possibly take."

I do my best to look stunned. "But five thousand rupees is the most I can possibly pay."

Amit is gravely wounded. "Ridiculous!" His coterie laughs aloud at my offer. "Surely we can come to an agreement."

"Surely."

"I will accept eighteen thousand from you, local from Chennai."

"For you, Amit, I would pay seven thousand."

He launches into a protracted speech about the quality of each item, the painstaking manufacturing process, etc., etc.

"For such good quality I can pay eight thousand. But no more."

"I am a fair man. I will accept seventeen thousand."

"Carolyn, Lisa, I'm sorry but we're not getting anywhere here." They look at me in horror. I stand. "We'll come back another day."

Amit doesn't flinch. "It is decided. I will sell for fourteen thousand." He nods, and a woman begins to bag the items.

"I will happily pay you ten thousand, but not one rupee more."

Amit regards me in stony silence. "Please wait, my boss will come."

Attendants carry an ancient man into the room and set him in front of me on the floor. His ears are enormous, his head bald. He bears a striking resemblance to Yoda. Amit speaks in his ear. The old man whispers in Tamil. Amit nods.

"My boss says ten thousand is too low."

"Could you give me that pad of paper, please?"

I draw a picture like this:

The patriarch smiles. He returns the paper with "twelve thousand" written across the bottom. I draw this:

He then retorts:

He writes "eleven thousand, five hundred," to which I respond:

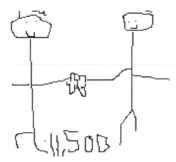

The old man becomes a grinning Yoda bobble-head doll. We shake hands while his helpers wrap the already wrapped silks in several more layers.

"But what about the other items?" Amit asks, nodding at the leftovers.

"We don't really want them, and besides, we don't have time to negotiate."

Carolyn's grip tightens on my arm. I wave dismissively. "Thank you, anyway."

We walk to the car with Carolyn and Lisa looking dejected.

Amit follows. "But saar!"

I put one leg in the Jeep. "I'll tell you what. You gave us almost a forty-five percent discount on the items we bought. If you'll give us the same on those items we don't need, I'll buy them just to make the ladies happy. But we're in a hurry. I need a 'yes' or a 'no.'"

Amit struggles to contain himself; the urge to bargain is strong. "Yes! Yes," he blurts finally. "You have a deal." For a moment I think he's going to give me a bro-hug. Everything is wrapped up in an instant. "Good-bye, my friend. Please come again."

CHAPTER 14: TOO GHOST FOR COMFORT

THERE ISN'T MUCH FOR US on Indian TV, and the cable company does everything it can to keep it that way. The "cable company" consists of a slick salesman and his two cousin-brothers who splice off a piece of wire from who-knows-where, string the cable through the tops of our mango trees—they actually climb into the trees—and then run it through a hole they drill in our wall where they think our TV ought to go. Our "free" installation turns out not to be so free when they drill through a water pipe.

Once everything is up and running, our channels change location at random. For example, in the morning we might watch the Hot! Romance Channel on channel 5. By noon we have to tune into channel 21 for the same. By the end of the day HRC might be found on channel 62. And even though we religiously pay our three dollars per month, service is frequently interrupted, and any storm means a couple of days of waiting for the guys to re-string the cable through the trees.

On a Friday night I'm in my underwear half-watching *Back to the Future* dubbed into Tamil when the cable goes out again. It's midnight, I can't sleep, and I had just finished a biography of Che Guevara. (He was kind of a jerk.) I need some excitement. I slip outside and tiptoe behind the servants' quarters. (This is before I learned of the cobras in the backyard.)

"Ooooo," I moan, ghostlike, below Shanthi's window, "ooooo." I run back inside.

In the morning I find Dinesh, Shanthi, Shanthi's children, the microwave repairman, the security guard, a neighbor's servant, and the door-to-door fruit seller all standing around in my kitchen looking as if the sky were falling.

"What's the matter? Microwave broken again?"

"Microwave not broken, saar," Shanthi replies grimly.

"Then why is the microwave guy in here drinking my tea again?"

"Because it is teatime, saar."

"No, that's not what I mean. Why is he...oh, never mind. Is there something wrong?"

Shanthi tells the story of a strange noise she heard the previous night while preparing for bed.

"It is ghost, saar."

"Don't worry about it. It was probably just a thief."

"No, saar. This was not a people."

Shanthi explains that a ghost has been haunting our property for decades. Our gardener, Narayanan, who was "second boy" on our property about a hundred years ago, energetically bobbles his head in agreement.

"Do not laugh, saar." Shanthi is dead serious. "It is dangerous if you do not believe."

She reminds me our stereo has a strange habit of turning on by itself, which I have to admit is kind of creepy.

"My family sleeping all night with lights on. I cannot go outside in this morning before sun is coming up. I am very afraid, saar."

Narayanan begins to chant. I look to Dinesh for reason.

"You don't believe this mumbo jumbo, do you?"

Dinesh looks uncertain. "Please be careful, saar."

I decide I'd better fess up before things get really out of hand. "It was me! I made the noise. Ha, ha, ha. Gotcha!"

It doesn't sink in right away.

"Like this." I cup my hands to my mouth. "Ooooo, ooooo…"

It sinks in. Shanthi grabs a skillet, and I make a run for it out the back door. I avoid her until lunchtime, when, getting hungry, I decide I'd better make amends.

I wait until she is alone and poke my head in the kitchen. "You're not still mad at me, are you?"

"I'm not angry at master, saar," she lies. "I know noise is not really you. You smart man. You say it is saar so other servants not be afraid."

I give her a conspiratorial wink. "Maybe. And don't call me 'master.'"

✿✿✿

The phone rings after lunch. "Hello, how is your family?" Harish rasps.

"They're fine, Harish. Thank you."

"Your mother? Her health is good?"

"Thank you. Yes."

"And your father? He is fine?"

Each time Harish calls, he spends several minutes inquiring about the welfare of my household. If I try to get him to the point of his call—often there is no point except to inquire about our welfare—he simply ignores me and continues with his line of questioning. I was impatient with this when I first arrived in India, but I've learned to appreciate the way Harish operates.

"And Shanthi? She is fine?"

"Yes, she's doing great."

"And Dinesh, he is happy? His health is good?"

"Super. He gives his regards."

After Harish finishes, I inquire as to the welfare of his family and friends. I challenge myself to outdo him. After five minutes or so, when the good health of every single person we know in common has been determined, I ask him how I can help him.

"I will be at your house in five minutes only."

"Uh, OK. Where're we headed?"

"You will see. I will pick you up in my car." He hangs up.

Harish's father moved the family from the northern state of Gujarat to Chennai in the 1940s and made his fortune in the wholesale food business. Harish eventually took over the business, and now he supplies many of the best hotels in India with everything from rice to imported gourmet items. His supermarket occupies the ground floor of a multi-story building, and the remaining floors house his warehouse and distribution center. It is this operation he wants us to see.

We ride a freight elevator to the top floor, and Harish gives Dana, Cole, and me the tour as we wend our way back down via the stairs. A small army of workers sits on each floor, sorting rocks and chaff from lentils, beans, and rice by hand. A great many of these people have physical handicaps.

"Why are so many people in your office handicapped?" Cole asks, holding Harish's hand.

"It is the right thing if I hire them. Otherwise, they will not find work. And these people work very hard."

This mind-set is refreshing. I'd already noticed Harish's high-caste birth never stops him from treating all around him with respect. He makes a point to treat our servants warmly and politely. He always greets them when he comes to see us and enquires about their welfare often. Harish tells me that Shanthi and Dinesh are good people whom we can trust to take care of us. We agree with him.

❋❋❋

Not long after the "ghost" incident, Cole, Dana, and I head home to Texas for what the State Department calls "rest and relaxation." Since Chennai is considered a "hardship" post, once during our two-year assignment the department gives us a trip either home or to a regional R&R point. Since my parents are distraught we've taken their grandson so far away, we have no choice but to spend our R&R in Texas instead of Australia or Paris, which is where many of Dana's colleagues go. It's kind of early for us to be taking our R&R since we're not yet through our first year in India, but we're timing our vacation to coincide with an opportunity for me to take the oral component of the Foreign Service exam for a second time.

An Indian friend asks us to deliver a package to a relative in Texas. Of course, we cannot say no. That is simply not done. The package is delivered, sealed, to our door as we are preparing to leave.

"Do you think we ought to open that package?" I ask on the way to the airport.

"It could be a bomb, saar," Dinesh says.

"Yeah, or drugs," Dana adds.

Cole pounds on the package. "It's probably *solid gold*!"

It is kind of heavy. "All right. Give it here." I open the package and find several jars of mango pickles.

Heaven smiles on us, because as soon as we get on the plane, Cole falls asleep and stays that way throughout a three-hour takeoff delay and the entire eight-hour flight to Belgium. We change planes to Belgium-based Sabena. They feed us.

"Is this chicken or some kind of weird bean?" Dana asks. "It's no wonder they're going bankrupt."

Dana contends her favorite airline food was had during a trip to we once took to Thailand on Pakistan International Airlines, and I must admit it tasted good. I took issue, however, with the number of flies circling my meal and the flight attendants' brawl in the aisle. (Really!) It also didn't help that there was only one operating bathroom on the very crowded plane—I think some people didn't actually have seats—and that we ran out of toilet paper shortly after takeoff.

Anyway, as I sit shoehorned into my seat on Sabena, trying to figure out if what I'm eating is meat or a dinner roll, I'm thinking I've had enough of planes and traveling altogether. State Department regs dictate we fly the cheapest carrier for every leg of our journey back to Texas, so we have to travel on four different airlines, which wreaks havoc on my attempt to accumulate frequent-flyer miles on any single airline. So much for rest and relaxation. We almost die getting out of Washington, DC, on United: flat tire, fuel leak, and climate control system failure. The pilot comes over the PA system and says—I swear—"It seems like we've got some serious problems with this plane." It's amazing he's able to ever get us off the ground.

Yet this pales in comparison to the risks I've been taking within India. I hate flying, and much more so on airlines known to have a poor safety record.

"But you've flown all over the world. You ought to be used to it," a friend says.

"On the contrary, I don't like to fly *because* I've flown all over the world. I've seen some crazy stuff."

At any rate, I don't really have a fear of flying at all. I have a fear of plummeting uncontrollably toward the ground at hundreds of miles an hour. That's what scares me, and, unfortunately, my job at Dell India requires me to fly almost every week. I try as much as possible to fly on Jet Airways, but sometimes I get stuck on Air India or Indian Airlines, two airlines notable for surly staff and Paleolithic aircraft. Once, while on the tarmac in New Delhi, my plane filled with a thumping noise so loud the passengers and flight attendants had to cover their ears. Otherwise, they appeared unperturbed.

"Excuse me," I shouted to a flight attendant above the din. "Shouldn't we be alarmed by this noise?"

"You've never flown Indian Airlines, have you?" she snarled and hastily moved away.

America is sublime; we've only been in India seven months but already home feels like Mars. Everything is so clean and orderly. Restaurant food is bland, and the portions are enormous. Dinner— and the check—arrives disconcertingly quick.

"Can't we even sit and talk a while?" I wonder aloud. We also notice our country has an obesity problem.

Everybody's too busy to stop and talk. People say, "Hi, how are you?" without really wanting an answer. Everyone drives so fast and gets bent out of shape at the slightest affront.

"You can't pull right out in front of people, honey," Dana reminds me.

"I don't see why not. The world's not going to end if they have to slow down a little."

The State Department allows us to put together a "consumables" shipment while on R&R—household items for shipment back to India—and so we go to the grocery store. Amazing. Aisles upon aisles of corn chips (forty-six varieties), gummy candy (thirty-four), beef jerky (140), olive oil (123) and things like organic apple-cinnamon cider vinegar drink and mesquite BBQ roasted broad bean crisps with sea salt. Do we really need all this? In the end, we buy things Americans truly do better, like potato chips and toilet paper.

Before we head back to India, I pop up to Washington, DC, to take the Foreign Service oral examination again. I have already passed the written exam a second time, and I'm confident; Dana has prepped me for weeks. I fail again, and I can't help but wonder if someone is trying to tell me something. I curse the State Department all the way back to Chennai.

We return from a month away to find Dinesh waiting for us as at the airport. It's a clear, sunny day.

"It's great to see you, Dinesh," I say, shaking his hand, and I mean it.

"You too, sir and madam and Cole."

As when we first arrived in Chennai, the odors of India assault our noses—diesel exhaust, fried snacks, body odor, spices—and the scene is chaotic. Men fight to carry our suitcases, taxi drivers chase us, vendors aggressively proffer their goods. This time we casually ignore them and follow Dinesh to the Jeep in the VIP parking space at the airport's front door. Even Cole looks jaded. As we leave the airport, a man stands by the highway selling red balloons for two rupees each—about five US cents. No one pays him any heed. I wonder how much money he could possibly make and then cringe to think that small amount of money is worth his while to stand there all day. As we cross the Adyar River, I watch women washing their clothes in the filthy water among the water buffaloes. Arriving at The Flame, we find the security guard asleep and the locks cut off the gates of our compound. Welcome home.

Construction of the mansion next door has progressed rapidly in our absence. A foundation has been laid. Women carry bricks on their heads—I count fourteen on one head—to men who lay them. (The bricks, not the women, silly.)

"You're not a real woman unless you can carry at least ten bricks on your head," I remark to Dana.

These very real women manage to balance bricks on their heads and keep their saris wrapped modestly around them at the same time. They use all sorts of things to cushion their heads: old shirts, straw...*my underwear.*

"Shanthi," I ask, "why is there a woman at the construction site next door with a pair of my underwear on her head?"

"Because bricks, they hurt her head, saar."

"Let me rephrase the question: How did the woman get a pair of my underwear?"

"I have no idea, saar. Very strange."

CHAPTER 15: CATCH AND POLICE

OUR FAITHFUL FRIEND, KIM, VISITS from Texas. She is an unapologetic professional student, bouncing from advanced degree program to advanced degree program in search of infinite wisdom. She keeps garden gnomes in the trunk of her car for photo ops, holds elaborate funerals for her cats, and always falls head over heels for the wrong guy. We'd issued a standing invitation to visit to all our friends, and we are pleasantly surprised when Kim takes us up on it.

Kim helps me and Cole sort toys to carry to a local orphanage run by Mother Theresa's Sisters of Charity organization. Cole got so many toys for Christmas that our playroom is bursting at the seams; even he agrees there are too many.

"If you haven't touched it in a year, it needs to go," I say to Cole as he sorts his toys.

"That's sound resonabubbly."

"Reasonable."

"Yeah, that's what I said. Reasonabobble."

"OK."

The orphanage houses children who are most likely not going to be adopted by anyone: children with missing limbs, other unsightly birth defects, or severe mental handicaps. Cleft palates are the least of the problems among these children who are typically abandoned at the orphanage's door. Conditions are Spartan, to say the least, but the facilities are clean and the children seem well cared for. A nun gives us a tour of the orphanage, and I worry this might be too much for Cole, who is now almost four, to handle.

He asks a lot of questions, which I answer as best I can. He sees babies with no arms or legs and children who lay in bed thrashing and moaning. I feel strongly that my child should understand the world around him, but I know I'm pushing the envelope. I want to shield him from this at such a tender age, but I want him to see the beauty of the compassion exhibited by women who have dedicated their lives to these children.

Cole sits between Kim and me in the backseat of the Jeep on the way home from the orphanage.

"Daddy, why does God make people with handicaps?"

"I don't know. Maybe to teach the rest of us how to be compassionate."

"Daddy, do I have a handicap?"

"Well, son, we all have handicaps. Some people's handicaps are just easier to see."

"Do you have a handicap?"

"Well, no severe handicaps like what we saw today."

"What is one of your handicaps?"

"Well, I can't see very well at all without glasses, and I'm terrible at math."

"What's my handicap?"

"I don't know. What do you think?"

Cole bursts into tears. "I don't have any handicaps! I don't!"

I want to tell him, "You're the most perfect little boy in the whole world. I love you so much." Instead, I hold him tight and let him cry.

✳✳✳

I take some time off to give Kim the tour of Chennai. There aren't a whole lot of sights of interest to tourists in Chennai, and, with Dinesh driving, we hit them all in a day. A large cohort of the infirm and elderly sits at the entrance of the amazing Kapaleeshwarar Temple in the Mylapore neighborhood. They are not begging; they are simply waiting with their empty bowls. Just feet away from these folks vendors hawk simple lunches of rice and dal from their mobile kitchens. Diners sit on plastic stools, scooping the hot mixtures into their mouths with their fingers.

"I wish there was something we could do," Kim mumbles.

"It is custom, ma'am and saar," Dinesh says, "to buy lunch for these people, if you wish. This is why they are waiting here at the temple."

"Oh. How does it work?" I ask.

"You pay the man selling food, and he will give to them."

"Oh, yes, of course, we'll buy them some food. How much is it?"

Dinesh speaks to a vendor in Tamil, and then "Fifteen rupees one person, saar," he says to me.

About thirty US cents. Thinking of the twenty-dollar meal we had with Kim the night before, I hand Dinesh a wad of rupees. "OK. Please take care of it, Dinesh. Thank you." Kim and I remove our shoes and enter the temple complex.

After Mylapore we visit the busy shopping district of Pondy Bazaar and browse the modest hardware, clothing, and kitchenware shops, trailed by an entourage of urchins. They touch our forearms again and again, asking for money, as we window-shop.

"Food, saar, please five rupees," begs a barefoot girl dressed in rags.

"What should we do?" Kim asks.

I purse my lips. I've had occasion to think about this a lot; encountering people begging for food or money has been a near daily occurrence since arriving in India. "I prefer to donate to organizations that help the poor. I think that's how we can help the most."

"Well, do you mind if I give them something?"

"Of course not. I'll leave that up to you. But I can tell you that if you give her any money, these kids will *not* leave us alone until we leave."

The corners of Kim's mouth turn downward. Tears are welling in her eyes. "How can I do nothing with her standing right here in front of me?"

I squeeze Kim's hand. "When you go back home, these children are still going to be here whether you see them or not. Should it make a difference if they are standing here in front of you? Let me connect you with some charities that do a great deal of good."

Kim is considering this when two police officers—easily recognized by their feces-colored uniforms, hyperbolic mustaches, and third-trimester pot bellies—step in front of us. The children scatter.

"You are breaking the law," one of the officers announces to us.

I ignore him and begin walking, pulling Kim along. The policemen catch up and get in front of us again.

"Stop! You are breaking the law."

Once again we walk around them. Once again they get in front of us.

"Please stop. We only want to talk with you."

They point to a van on the side of the road marked "Mobile Police Station."

There are other police officers inside.

"We don't want to talk," I say. "Sorry."

"You must stop. We are the police."

"Have a nice day."

We walk briskly away as the policemen stare at our backs.

The Chennai police are frequently out trolling for cash in this manner. They often stand on the roadside motioning for every fourth vehicle or so to pull over. The word is that you certainly won't get away without some sort of "fine." The unofficial American Consulate position is that since the Chennai police typically have neither cars nor guns, anyone would be a fool to stop. So we never do.

※※※

"I have what they call 'secondary infertility,'" Dana sadly informs me after months of treatments and tests, meaning that no matter how often or how hard we try, we won't be having any more children naturally. (Nevertheless, we try.) I'm sad, too. Not so much because we can't have any more biological children, but because Dana's sad. To her, this feels like the end of the road. She can have surgery; that might do the trick, but there's certainly no guarantee. To me, it's simply time for Plan B.

Even before we got married I was interested in adoption. My roommate in college had a girlfriend, Ariane, with a much younger adopted sister from Haiti whom she occasionally brought around the guys' dorm with her on a weekend. I was fascinated by this little girl.

"Why did your parents adopt her when they already had kids of their own?" I asked, a stupid sophomore.

"The world is full of children who need homes," Ariane said. "You have no idea."

She was right; I had no idea.

At that moment the notion of adoption was planted like a seed in my mind. And when we get to India it *weighs* upon my mind. When I explain to Cole that the little girl his age carrying a naked baby and wading through choking traffic is not waving to him but rather begging him for food, when I shoo the children away in the market, when I see kids going through our garbage—it *weighs* upon my mind.

And so it is with a sense of destiny and even relief that I say to Dana, "The world is full of children who need homes. Why don't we help one of them?"

CHAPTER 16: SUICIDE MISSION

W HEN WE ARRIVE IN INDIA, applications for a US visa can still be made by mail, and reputable companies who need to send employees abroad for business purposes are able do so without much trouble. There are, however, bogus companies that exist to help unqualified Indians get a visa—for a fee. Typically, these firms provide a visa applicant with a letter confirming his or her employment at the company and explaining why the employee needs a visa for travel to the firm's US office. Often, these letters are written on such shoddy letterheads or the grammar is so bad that the American visa officer can dismiss them outright as a sham. However, separating the wheat from the chaff is not always easy, and, for this reason, someone from the consulate periodically makes unannounced visits to companies that sponsor large numbers of visa applicants or are otherwise under suspicion.

When it's Dana's turn to do antifraud investigations, she and one of the consulate's Foreign Service nationals—government-speak for a local employee—head to Hyderabad, a city with the dubious distinction as the visa fraud capital of South India. Dana and her FSN show up at businesses with names like "Info-Tech Systems, Inc." and ask to see personnel files to verify that a particular visa applicant actually works there. Often they arrive to find a firm that has no legitimate need to send an employee to the US or that they have been given a false address altogether. Sometimes they end up at a *dosa* restaurant. Fortunately, Dana likes almost all food, including dosas. A dosa is sometimes described as an Indian pancake. It is *not* a pancake. It is more similar to a savory crepe and is uniquely South Indian and a kids' favorite.

While Dana is wreaking havoc in Hyderabad, I take Cole to school as usual one morning and then head to the consulate to mail a package and buy a Snickers at the commissary. I'm chatting with a friend about the upcoming volleyball game against the Russians—the Russians always win—when the consulate security chief phones and says I need to go home immediately as there has been an "incident."

Dinesh drives me slowly and carefully home, where I find a small army of consulate security guards, servants, construction workers from next door, and unknown passersby waiting as fast as they can for someone to tell them what to do. A guard informs me that in my absence six thugs showed up to beat some money out of Shanthi's good-for-nothing husband, Dom. Apparently, Dom likes to borrow money and gamble, and this time he lost big. Shanthi locked herself in the servants' quarters, and Narayanan, our four-foot-tall gardener, armed himself with a machete, locked himself in our house, and called the consulate. The six trespassers ran off when the consulate guards showed up. In other words, just a regular day in India.

First, I talk Narayanan out of the house and thank him for his vigilance.

"Well, where is Dom?" I ask the crowd.

Narayanan flashes a toothless grin and points to the sky. Cringing, I look up and find Dom, tears streaming down his face, standing on the edge of the roof as if ready to jump. This is going to be even more exciting than I expected.

Everybody looks at me as if I'm supposed to know what to do. Fine. I mount the ladder attached to the wall of our home and climb to the roof. Dinesh, after only a split second of hesitation, faithfully follows. With Dinesh translating, I explain to Dom that jumping off my roof would be very stupid because the fall would likely not be enough to kill him.

"If you think life sucks now, just imagine begging for alms at the temple for the next forty years."

Dom acts as if he doesn't understand a single word, but when I point to the ladder and shout, "Get your skinny butt off my roof," he goes down.

Nobody applauds my heroic efforts, although I suspect Dinesh would have if I had asked him. Shanthi races out of the servants' quarters and begins physically and verbally abusing Dom. Dinesh refuses to interpret her words for me, but I get the gist. We restrain her when she picks up a large rock.

The consulate's regional security officer, John, shows up. He is kind of a twit. His greatest accomplishment since arriving at post has been to force all consulate families to get consulate photo IDs for their children, no matter their age. State Department regulations don't require this, but—whatever—that's just Crazy John, and it gave Cole a nice souvenir. John chills out after six months or so, and he almost becomes likeable. But right now I need to get him out of my yard so I can deal with the situation.

"This family can no longer live on the premises," John announces. "They must vacate their quarters immediately."

Shanthi collapses in a heap on the ground. When she revives, it takes her and her sobbing kids about three minutes to get all their stuff out of the servants' quarters. Dom tries to help as he dodges Shanthi's blows. I feel horrid.

John very strongly suggests I fire Shanthi, and as regional security officer, he has overall authority for the security of the consulate, its property, and its personnel. To appease him I offer to suspend her without pay and bring her back only with conditions. I don't want to fire Shanthi; we get along well, and she's a hard worker. He reluctantly agrees to the suspension and leaves.

Shanthi assumes she's out of a job, and while her kids stand on the street with their belongings, she comes back to beg for forgiveness. I pull her into the kitchen and away from the large audience still standing in our yard. She drops to the floor and tries to touch my feet.

I pull her upright. "Would you stop that, please?"

"I will surely die, saar!"

"But—"

"I will divorce him, saar, if I can keeping job!"

"Shanthi—"

"My children will starving, saar!"

At least she doesn't tell me I'm possessed like Leela did.

"*Stop*! I'm not going to fire you!"

Shanthi stares at me in disbelief. Several times, I think she's going to say something, but no words come from her mouth. Finally, she drops into a plastic chair.

"You mean master not fire me?"

"Don't call me 'master.'"

"Saar not fire me?"

"Nope. I'm not going to fire you. You're suspended for a week."

Suspension, a concept she seems to have not encountered before, takes some time to sink in. I tell her under no circumstances is Dom ever allowed on the premises again. She can do anything she wants on her own time, but I had better not ever see Dom again.

"I divorce him!" Shanthi cries. "I hate all man!" She pauses for reflection. "Only not you, saar."

With that, she rips the necklace from her neck that symbolizes her marriage to Dom and throws it in the trash.

"Please don't be rash, Shanthi." I dig the necklace out of the trash. "I'll keep this until you come back, and then you can decide what to do with it."

She looks at me askance. "Saar not selling it?"

"Geez, no! I'm not going to sell it."

Shanthi finally leaves but not without asking several times if I'm only joking about not firing her.

"Don't be afraid. Your job will be waiting for you next week."

Shanthi's head bobbles slowly, and she shuffles out the door.

The gravity of the situation, however, doesn't sink in until Cole and I finish leftover spaghetti for lunch, and I realize the sink full of dishes is not going to wash itself.

"Just put them in the machine that washes the dishes," Cole says.

"We don't have one."

Cole stares a me a moment. "Oh," he drawls. "Well, then that's terrible."

"Yeah. Terrible."

The back door opens. Dinesh, having just washed the car, puts on an apron and begins washing the dishes without saying a word. Whew! I was worried for a moment there. I remind myself to give that man a raise.

Day 1

I QUICKLY FIND OUT THAT Dinesh is as good at doing dishes as Shanthi would be as a chauffeur. I get up the next morning and wash the damned dishes myself. Dinesh gingerly reminds me that morning tea and toast is part of his and the other servants' compensation packages. Narayanan, the gardener, stands at the back door shaking his teacup at me.

Morning and afternoon tea are elaborate rituals around which all schedules rotate and all meaningful work comes to a standstill. The household help find it very strange that I refuse to have tea with them, and they claim to fear for my health. This morning I realize that, although I'm a decent cook, I don't know how to make a pot of tea the way Indians like it. Between the two of us, Dinesh and I manage to make a passable pot without hurting anyone, and I try Indian *masala chai* for the first time—as much milk as tea, a ridiculous amount of sugar, cardamom, cloves, and cinnamon—and to my surprise I like it a lot. (Try it! Get this and other recipes at gregorybuford.com.)

We stumble through the greater part of the day without Shanthi, and then it dawns on me that I will to have to fix supper for the first time in nine months. A stranger in my own kitchen, I have trouble locating even the most basic items. I remember we still have some leftover spaghetti. Happy not to be defeated, I pop the spaghetti in the microwave, and—*boom!*—the microwave explodes in a flash of light. Dinesh, who has been sitting at the kitchen table listening to Cole read *The Cat in the Hat*, gets on the phone with the repairman.

"When is Shanthi coming back?" Cole asks. "She knows how to use the microwave."

I say things to him I'd rather not repeat. Dana calls to tell me what a wonderful time she is having in Hyderabad.

Day 2

I relearn how to use a washing machine and start my first load. I put on an apron and start in on a sink full of dishes. Dinesh loiters at the back door looking at his feet, afraid to remind me it's morning teatime. The microwave repairman calls to say he won't have spare parts for at least three days. I feel faint. Cole and I go to our favorite samosa stall for lunch and eat cold samosas for dinner. We eat on paper plates and drink from plastic cups.

Cole looks depressed. "Daddy, what does *suspended* mean?"

I explain the meaning of the word.

"Why did Shanthi suspend you?"

"Shut up, kid, and mop the floor," I say with a snarl.

Lying in bed that night I remember the load of clothes I forgot to take out of the washer.

Day 3

I begin to wonder if I hadn't been a little too harsh on Shanthi in suspending her for the week. Maybe a day would have sufficed to get John, the regional security officer, off my back. Too bad, anyway. I don't have any idea how to find her since she has no street address or telephone.

Dinesh knocks on the kitchen's screen door.

"Saar, shall I clean the kitchen?"

Cheeky bastard. "What's wrong with the kitchen? I cleaned it last night. Can't you see that?"

"No, saar," he replies, expressionless.

I have a good mind to fire him for that!

We pick up Cole from school at noon, and he gets invited to have lunch at a friend's. I wonder if I can join him. Instead, I go home alone and have toast. I resolve to go shopping, and it dawns on me that I have never actually been shopping in India. Of course, I have been to the expensive air-conditioned specialty store to buy things like mayonnaise and chocolate, but I have never bought, say, a vegetable. Things like that are bought by Shanthi in the real market.

"Dinesh, please take me to the place Shanthi shops for our food."

"Are you wanting I do it, saar?"

"Nah, I got this."

I leave the market feeling like a sucker; Shanthi never seemed to spend so much. Maybe my bargaining skills aren't so good after all. Riding home I remember the load of clothes I need to take out of the washer. We go out for dinner.

Day 4

I nurse my aching lower back as I wash dishes and then search in vain for lotion to soothe my dishpan hands. Cole sits at the kitchen table composing songs.

"Shanthi, Shanthi, please come back. Before my daddy breaks his back."

All I have to do is make it through the morning. Cole and I are taking the train in the afternoon to Hyderabad to join Dana for the weekend, and, hopefully, Shanthi will be back on Monday. I spend the morning preparing snacks for the train and packing. I'm irritated because, among everything else, I can't find my favorite pair of shorts. I get the lunch dishes washed, and Cole and I go upstairs to take a shower. We get undressed, step in the shower, turn the knob, and...no water! Dinesh hears me yell and comes running. He flatly informs me that Shanthi has not been around to order the water delivery this week. Luckily, Dinesh, God bless him, has taken the liberty of filling two large buckets with water in anticipation of just such an emergency.

How could I ever have thought of firing him? I remind myself again to give him a raise. Now almost late for the train, Cole and I run outside and bathe in the backyard as Dinesh pours water over us. All work halts at the construction site next door as the workers stop to gawk.

Dinesh gets us to the station just in time for the seventeen-hour ride to Hyderabad. As he waves good-bye from the platform—undoubtedly with relief—Cole learns that train seats are great for bouncing, and I remember the clothes in the washer.

CHAPTER 18: NUNS AND DAUGHTERS

COLE AND I TAKE THE overnight train to join Dana for the weekend in Hyderabad, where she has been all week conducting antifraud investigations, and then we'll all fly home together on Sunday. Amazingly, a one-way air ticket in India costs exactly half as much as a round-trip ticket, something we really take advantage of because we enjoy taking various modes of transportation as we travel throughout India. Clearly, some of the high-priced MBAs American carriers use to determine their pricing structure need to go over to India and tell those nuts that a one-way ticket is supposed to cost more than a round-trip ticket.

Hyderabad, as the crow flies, is not even that far from Chennai, but if you travel only twenty miles an hour and make several stops along the way, it takes a while to get there. On the train we sit next to a nice man, his shy wives, and innumerable children. Within seconds of our train's departure he explains he'd brought the family to Chennai to apply for US visas. Their visas were denied, and he wonders if I can do anything to help. I explain to him that since I am Canadian, I naturally hate all Americans and things American and can be of no help to him. He quickly loses interest in us.

We ride in third class, which is one microscopic step above ordinary class, if that means anything to you, because there are no other tickets available. When we finally find our correct berth, I whip out my steel cable and padlock our luggage to various parts of the train. The dozen people staring at us are duly impressed. I politely decline several offers of tea from passengers; I can't risk falling for the old drugs-in-the-tea trick, a well-known hazard on Indian trains. We open a care package Harish sent us for the trip and gorge on dry frosted flakes. Cole and I have to share a very narrow top berth during the night. It is nice to spoon him while he sleeps, but I hardly sleep at all, hanging halfway off the berth.

Twenty and some-odd hours later we inch into Hyderabad and make for the hotel to meet up with Dana. Long-distance train travel isn't feeling as romantic as it had sounded a few days earlier when I booked the tickets. I recover, however, and the three of us spend a fun weekend at relatively clean movie theaters, not eating in the same five restaurants and visiting remarkable Golkonda Fort with its wonderful sound-and-light show and lots of stinky bats.

We also make a trip to an orphanage recommended to us by a friend. Since we got the news that Dana couldn't conceive another child, we'd connected with two American Consulate families already in the process of adopting. We'd heard horror stories over the years of the lengthy wait and great expense of adoption. (Why does adoption have to cost fifteen thousand dollars anyway? I think somebody's getting rich.) We are thrilled to learn from our consulate friends that we can adopt while in India and greatly reduce the time and expense involved.

We joke that if three families at the American Consulate—out of fifteen—adopt, Chennai will gain a reputation within the State Department as the "adoption" post, much like Colombia is known for sending every single man home with a local wife, and Algeria is known for breaking up marriages and driving people insane. Incidentally, Port of Spain, capital of Trinidad and Tobago, is called "Port of Pain" for the consistently dysfunctional US embassy there.

At any rate, the first step is to visit the orphanage and talk with its chief, Sister Theresa.

We find the orphanage very clean, adequately staffed, and full of happy children. Sister Theresa, an endearing septuagenarian nun, makes up for her lack of efficiency and decent record-keeping with love for the children under her care. She considers it a trivial detail that Dana has not even made up her mind about adopting.

"You will adopt," she says, "because God has chosen you."

"In that case," I whisper to Dana, "it would be nice if God would change a few diapers."

Of great concern to us are persistent rumors of widespread baby buying and outright child abduction in the state of Andhra Pradesh, in which the orphanage lies. Officials at the American Consulate tell us some American families had their adoption cases suspended, pending investigations into the relinquishment of the babies in question. We raise this matter with Sister Theresa.

She tells us agents roam the countryside of the state offering relatively gigantic sums of money for girl babies who often aren't wanted by their poverty-stricken families. These agents target the poorest of the poor who find it difficult to resist sums as large as forty dollars. The babies are then sold to unscrupulous orphanages, which in turn offer the children to foreign couples who pay mandatory "donations" of thousands of dollars. Witnessing every day the poverty that exists in India, we can easily envision this scenario. Relatively rare but still a problem are kidnappings of children for sale to the same orphanages. Sister Theresa assures us she only accepts babies brought in by their parents for whom she pays only minimal travel expenses.

In the orphanage live approximately one hundred girls and three boys. Of the boys, two of them are severely handicapped. Many in India still consider girls of lower value than boys, which accounts for India's nasty female infanticide problem and likely the disproportionate number of girls in the orphanage. We spend the afternoon playing with the babies, which has the desired effect upon Dana.

"Well, I guess we can do this," she says to me when we get home. She looks worried, not happy.

"What's wrong?"

"Well…well…I kind of don't want to say it. But, I'm just…worried," she stammers.

"What? What is it?"

Dana begins to cry. "Well, what if…I'm just afraid that…well, you see, with Cole, I just love him so much. I'm afraid that I might not feel the same about an adopted child. Is that terrible? I mean…we were with Cole since the very beginning. It might not be the same. Does that mean I'm horrible?"

I wrap my arms around her. "No. It means you're human. Anyway, it won't be the same, but you will love her just as much as you love Cole. That, I know."

"'Her'? Does that mean it's going to be a girl?"

"I guess so."

"OK," she squeaks. "Let's do it."

We tell Cole, and he is beside himself with the anticipation of having a sibling. I call Sister Theresa and let her know we're in.

"Of course, you are," she says. "God is great." She promises to get back to us soon with the next steps in the process.

***

It is not long after we make this momentous decision that I come up with my next brilliant idea. Things at work have steadily deteriorated since the Australia trip. I spend a great deal of time on the road, and both my boss and the head of Dell India, who acts like my boss, want me to travel even more. If we are going to have a new child at home, I want to be around to raise her and not leave that extremely important job to a hired hand with different values.

"I want to quit my job."

Dana knows me well, and so my proposal doesn't entirely surprise her. "Why?"

"Work sucks, but that's not it. I want to take care of the children. I don't want to be gone all the time. I don't want the kids raised by someone else. And the adopted baby is going to need extra attention."

Dana looks at me the way she does when she's about to tell me she loves me. "For how long? Like, forever?"

"I don't know."

"OK," she says with a smile, "but let's use up your vacation time first."

So before leaving Dell and adopting a baby, we take a vacation. Look out, Rome!

CHAPTER 19: WHEN IN ROME, EAT GELATO!

SHANTHI ARRIVES THE MORNING AFTER we return from Hyderabad and scrapes the molded remains of my shorts out of the washing machine.

She gives me a dirty look. "Saar is not knowing how to take clothes out of washing machine?"

"Oh, yeah. I guess I forgot about those."

I give her back her betrothal necklace, which has a sizeable hunk of gold attached, and she never mentions Dom again. That is, until I go to jail, but that's another chapter.

The reader may recall that I accidentally purchased at a charity auction a single ticket to Europe on Lufthansa. Dell's "use it or lose it" vacation policy and the looming expiration date of the ticket mean that we take the trip in the first week in October. Since I'm planning to leave my job, we can't afford for Dana and Cole to fly in business class with me or even on the same airline, so Dana and Cole have the pleasure of flying Air Lanka, and, no, I hadn't heard of it either. The cheapest flight from Chennai to Europe is on Air Lanka and to Rome, so that's how we decide where to go on our trip. I feel really bad that Dana and Cole will travel in Cattle Class, enjoying whatever culinary oddities Air Lanka offers, and will have to lay over for a night in Sri Lanka before joining me in Italy. But it is what it is.

We are by this time familiar with the monsoon season in India, but we have no idea there is also one in Italy; it rains every day of our ten-day visit. Despite the rain, Rome is predictably fabulous. The air is clean(er), the food is as different from Indian as you can get, and Italian just sounds so cool. We eat gelato twice a day and hang out with the ten billion other tourists on the Spanish Steps. (Does anybody actually *live* in Rome?) And Italy is a kid's paradise; what child doesn't love pizza, pasta, and panini?

We have a brief moment of excitement on a bus when Dana believes someone is snatching her purse. She attacks the person nearest, a rather stooped senior citizen, not stopping until she has evicted him from the bus. (Dana has rather forcefully suggested I inform the reader that the bus was indeed stopped when she booted the little old man.)

After a few days in Rome we rent a car and drive to the spectacular Amalfi Coast. By the way, all those stories you've heard about the crazy drivers in Italy were obviously told by people who have never been to India. Trust me: There's no comparison. We rent a cliff-side suite in Conca dei Marini overlooking the Tyrrhenian Sea. I discover *limoncello*, and we eat our weight in *scialatielli ai frutti di mari*—fresh local pasta and seafood—and *'ndunderi*, a local ricotta gnocchi.

"So, do you forgive me for buying the plane ticket at the auction?" I ask Dana. We are sitting at a table on a cobbled street in front of an artisanal bakery.

She can't speak because she is wolfing down a *sfogliatella*, a flaky pastry filled with lemon cream. She nods in mute assent.

"Great. I forgive you for doubting me. Just don't do it again."

On our way back to Rome we visit Pompeii and climb the still-active volcano, Mount Vesuvius, that buried it back in the day and stop only long enough in Naples to sample a pizza Margherita in its birthplace.

Refreshed by our vacation, we return to Chennai and find our lady friends at the construction site next door still carrying piles of bricks on their heads. Now, however, they are carrying them to the second floor of the building, balancing across wooden planks on bamboo scaffolding. A group of lean, muscular men toil with a hand-cranked mixer, combining sand, gravel, and cement to make concrete, which the women also carry up the scaffolding for the men to use.

The gravel-makers amaze me the most: A truck arrives with a load of gray rocks—small boulders, actually—and women pound on them—*chink, chink, chink*—until they are reduced to gravel, stopping only for tea and a little lunch at midday. That *chink, chink, chink* will remain with me for as long as I remember India. At first it drives me nuts, and I discover I can't close enough windows and doors to drown out the noise. After a month or so, however, I begin to anticipate each blow of the hammer, and an interruption in their rhythm brings me to the window to see what's the matter.

Speaking of noise, India is a darn noisy place. Visit one of millions of small villages across India, and, at any time of day or night, the local temple, shrine, or mosque may decide everyone needs to enjoy its music or propaganda at intolerable levels. At Indian weddings, music is often played so loud that no one could possibly enjoy themselves, let alone talk to someone.

And it's not just India; many Asian countries seem full of the nearly deaf. Go to a public park in China, and just when you sit down for a quiet tea by a willow-lined lake, a loudspeaker will blast distorted, ear-splitting music. Staying in a mid-range hotel in Vietnam is like going to an all-night dorm party with every door wide open, music blasting, and revelers racing up and down the hall

all night. Even when we lived in polite Japan, there was nothing impolite about an elementary school blaring classical music over loudspeakers for three or four hours a day, making it impossible for its neighbors to hear their televisions.

✿✿✿

Not long after we return from Italy, Dinesh hears from a friend who owns an auto repair shop. The friend tells Dinesh that Dom, Shanthi's faux-suicidal deadbeat ex-husband, has come into his shop recently trying to sell some foreign auto parts. Dom also tells the shop owner that Dinesh has been fired and that he, Dom, is now our driver. Suspecting the parts are hot, the shop owner doesn't buy but instead notifies Dinesh, who, in turn, notifies me. Since imported auto parts are not readily available in India, I had brought some spares with us that I keep locked in a storage closet in the servants' quarters. A quick inspection reveals a break-in and missing spare parts.

"And where are my Adidas sandals that I keep at the back door?" Dana asks. "They've been missing since we got back from Rome."

I shrug. "Maybe I should've just let Dom jump off the roof."

Dinesh bobbles his head noncommittally.

Thrilled at the prospect of adventure, Dinesh, Cole, and I hop in the Jeep and head to the local police substation. It's packed. Angry men argue loudly, children are sleeping on the floor, it stinks of urine. But when we walk in you can hear a pin drop. Two middle-aged mustachioed men in diarrhea-brown uniforms are lounging behind desks stacked four feet high with yellowed, decaying paperwork. They drop their jaws and stare at me. A Raj-era ceiling fan slowly stirs the dust. Dinesh discreetly mentions to them my connection to the US consulate, and we are taken immediately to their superior.

I describe for the superior officer the missing items, including Dana's Adidas sandals, and my reasons for suspecting Dom. He twirls his long mustache, pats his ample belly, and dismisses with an impatient smile my offer to provide additional evidence.

"He is not needing evidence, saar," Dinesh interprets. "He only wants to know what to do with Dom when the parts are recovered."

Interesting. "What are my options?"

"You can ask only for return of missing property, or you can ask for return of missing property and punishment of the criminal."

"Punishment?" I like the sound of that. "What exactly does he have in mind?"

"He says, 'minimum three-month sentence.' As you wish, saar."

I walk across the room to the station's one cell. A wretched man with long matted hair and beard sits on the floor in the filth that has overflowed from the hole-in-the-floor toilet in the center of the cell. He is handcuffed behind his back. There are no chairs, no bed.

"Why does this man have no clothes?"

"They think maybe he is hiding something, saar."

"I see. Will Dom get a trial?"

Dinesh confers with the officer. "Boss says of course there will be a trial. *Eventually*. But the criminal must wait here until the trial begins. Minimum three months awaiting trial, saar."

Although I find the notion of having Dom punished quite appealing, I feel this punishment doesn't fit the crime.

"Just get me the parts," I say.

Two plainclothes detectives are assigned to the case. We find them reclining on the floor in another room, looking as if they have spent a career perfecting their air of utter apathy. When their boss barks at them in Tamil, however, they move their rears. I relay the story again for the detectives, and we move out. Outside, the detectives stop at the curb and stare at me.

"Uh, why are they looking at me like that?" I ask Dinesh.

"They are asking, saar, how you want the investigation to begin."

"I don't get it."

"You see, saar, they have no vehicle. They want to know if they will go with us in your vehicle, saar, or if you will provide them money to go by auto-rickshaw."

Of course. What was I thinking? "Sure. They can ride with us. This is going to be fun."

"Yes, saar."

Cole cries bloody murder as we drop him off at the house. "I want to go! I want to gooooooo," he wails.

"Sorry, pal. Not this time."

"Can I go next time?"

"Sure. The next time we have to go with the police to find Dom, you can go. I promise."

Shanthi tells the police where Dom and his extended family live—"Take him to prison, saar! I am not caring about that man."—but the cops are more interested in the Jeep and can't stop caressing its lines.

Not surprisingly, Dom is not home, and his relatives act as if they haven't seen him since childhood. I'm asked to wait in the car while the police have a word. When the cops come back, Dinesh explains that Dom's family was told that all the items must be at my house by four o'clock that afternoon or all of them, Grandma included, would have to report to the substation for questioning and remain there until Dom produced the goods.

"Well, I don't really want y'all to arrest his grandmother."

The cops' heads bobble in sync.

We go back to the house and wait over masala tea and toast, listening to Dinesh translate our police friends' fantastic tales of fighting crime in Chennai. Dom shows up at 3:30 with all the parts, the Adidas sandals, and a stupid smile on his face. He presents my auto parts as if he were giving me a gift and asks for a job. Leaving empty-handed, he says some obscenity under his breath, and the police have to step in to keep gentle Dinesh from pounding him. I provide small monetary tokens of my appreciation to the detectives, and Dinesh drives them back to the substation.

***

Dinesh invites us to his brother's wedding, and this is exactly the kind of cultural experience we have been waiting for. He advises me as I buy my first *dhoti*—a formal version of the laborer's wrap-skirt-like *lungi*, and a thigh-length cotton shirt with a mandarin collar. Cole gets a miniature version. White with a gold border, my dhoti constantly threatens to fall to my ankles, and so I cheat by securing it with a belt concealed under my shirt. After all, it won't do to flash the wedding party. Dana claims to find my dhoti quite sexy, and she has me wear it on other formal as well as private occasions. She wears a *salwar kameez*—a long, loose-fitting tunic top worn over drawstring pants, which is not designed to suit tall pale redheads, but she doesn't look half as bizarre as I do.

The wedding is a chaotic high-volume affair with hundreds of people crowding an un-air-conditioned hall to pay their respects to the happy couple. We risk upstaging the bride and groom when we arrive in our local garb and are received like royalty. Despite our objections, Dinesh assigns several of his friends as our handlers, and it makes for a ridiculous display of typical over-the-top Indian hospitality.

Our minders usher us to the dining area, where we find our place settings consist of large rounds of banana leaf. Attendants arrive and cover our leaves with a giant pile of rice, onto which are ladled several soupy dishes that we are expected to scoop up and eat with our hands. Upon noticing our hesitation, one of Dinesh's cousins races off to find spoons for the prissy foreigners. Determined to be good sports, we ball up the rice with our hands, South Indian-style, and try scooping food into our mouths without spilling it on our fancy clothes. (Any South Indian will tell you food simply doesn't taste right unless it is eaten with the hands, much the same that Japanese will say rice must be eaten with chopsticks.)

The hundred-degree heat and the close scrutiny start me sweating, and before long my shirt is soaking wet. Cole drops rice and lentil soup in his lap, and there are no napkins with which to wipe our food-covered hands. Just as we eat a respectable amount and plan to retreat to the bathrooms to clean up, Dinesh's cousin returns, beaming, with three spoons. Not to disappoint him, we eat a little more and then make a hasty escape to the facilities. We resolve to bring our own wet wipes next time.

After the wedding, Dinesh explains to me that his sister stands next in line to get married. Only after she weds will it be appropriate for his parents to begin the search for his bride. Dinesh desperately wants to get married, but finding a girl on his own and going on a date is something he simply cannot do. Much too shy, Dinesh will rely on his parents to find the right woman for him, though he claims his parents will accept any woman he chooses if he happens to meet one on his own.

I have begun teaching Dinesh how to use one of my old Dell laptops the company left with me when they issued me a new one. He enrolls in a keyboarding course at his own expense, and I start giving him projects to do, of which he is extremely proud. I introduce Dinesh to the internet, and he immediately realizes its practical applications when I show him some Indian matchmaking sites. He eventually establishes his own email account and spends his free time in internet cafés writing to new friends around the world.

Speaking of email, by this time I'm not even reading mine from work anymore. Arguments between my boss in Singapore and the head of Dell India over what I'm supposed to do have gotten out of hand. Shortly after we get back from Rome, I get a call from my boss, the same one who wouldn't talk to me in Australia.

"Greg, just don't do anything."

"Don't do anything?"

"Don't make any phone calls, don't do any traveling, and especially don't talk to that little prick in Dell India until we sort this out."

If I have any lingering doubts about my future with Dell, this erases them all. So I do as he says and turn my attention elsewhere: Halloween.

D ANA AND I ARE NOT VISUALLY creative people. Our friend Kim—the one who travels with garden gnomes—describes us as aesthetically impaired. We have never successfully decorated a home; our little yellow house in Texas had almost nothing on the walls, and the end tables sat bare. When we sold it after a year, it looked as if we'd just moved in. Likewise, in ten long years of marriage, we've never once been able to come up with decent Halloween costumes. So when we get invited to the consulate Halloween party—costumes mandatory—we are worried.

"I can't be a nerd again this year," I say. "I just can't."

"How about a ghost? We can get an old bedsheet."

"That's pathetic. I'm going to talk to Dinesh."

I explain to Dinesh the notion of Halloween and our predicament.

"Of course, saar. I will take care."

I'm skeptical. "We'd better be ready with plan B," I tell Dana.

"How can we be ready with plan B when we don't even have plan A?"

The next day Dinesh brings Dana a portrait of the Hindu goddess Meenakshi Amman.

"What does madam think?"

The green-skinned goddess sports a red silk outfit of indescribable complexity: a skirt with more than thirty pleats and a half-dozen gold necklaces, bangles, earrings, nose rings, and cheek rings. She is crowned with a two-foot-tall jewel-encrusted headdress over her waist-length jet-black hair.

Dana is in awe. "This is it. This is it! I'll win the contest for sure."

Dammit. She's right—if they can pull it off. "Dinesh, how are you going to turn her into that?"

"Movie magic, saar. Movie magic."

✾✾✾

India makes more movies than any country in the world, and Chennai makes more movies than any place in India, including Bombay's Bollywood. Indians love movies, and for us the twenty-five-cent tickets are worth it for the cultural experience alone. The shows play at deafening volumes to drown out the noise of children running in the aisles, adults conversing loudly, and mobile-phone users shouting to be heard. It is truly a carnival atmosphere. Since all Indian movies are musicals with roughly the same star-crossed-lovers plot, it's not necessary to speak the language to figure out what's happening on-screen. Chennai churns out these movies at an alarming rate at the many film studios around town, and Dinesh's plan is to take Dana to one of these studios and find a costume designer that can make her a goddess.

"You're just going to drive up to a studio and ask for a costume designer?" I ask. "Yeah, like that's going to work."

"Yes, saar. We will succeed, saar."

"Ha. Good luck with that."

"Thank you, saar."

Of course, Dinesh is right; when he shows the costume designer the portrait of Meenakshi Amman, the designer simply bobbles his head, takes measurements, and remarks that Dana will need a wig as well. We go next to a jeweler and rent the necessary finery for Dana's hair, wrists, toes, nose, and ears. Finally, Dinesh arranges for a movie makeup artist to come to the house and turn her green on the appointed day. Dana is ecstatic. I am despondent.

I pull Dinesh aside. "Listen, pal, whose side are you on anyway?"

"I am on madam's side, saar."

"You could've at least lied."

Dinesh takes me to a bustling market on the north side of town where official police uniforms can be bought for a song. For less than ten bucks I'm transformed into an authentic chief inspector, including hat, whistle, pistol (toy), holster, nightstick, and all the relevant buttons, badges, and medals. An enormous crowd of onlookers gathers to watch as I try on the uniform in the open air.

I look at myself in a cracked mirror. "Do you reckon this is legal?"

Dinesh's head bobbles.

"Yeah, that's what I thought." At any rate, it's by far the best costume I've ever had before or since. "Well, whatever. Now I'm a cinch to win the contest."

"No, saar. Madam will win."

On Halloween the makeup guy shows up to paint Dana. It looks awesome.

"What do you think's in this stuff?" she asks, eyeing her dark-green skin.

"Lead. Lots of lead," I say. "But don't worry. It'll probably wash off. Just tell me if you get dizzy."

The tailor dresses her. Dana dons her waist-length wig, crown, and jewels. Wielding her scepter and standing more than seven feet tall with crown, Dana looks like she's just stepped off a movie set. Darn. My best costume ever, and I'm going to lose to my wife. Indeed, no one is even close. Dana wins the costume contest, and, as usual, I can only bask in her glow. They did throw me a little bone, designating me "most authentic."

Before we went to the party, we asked our Indian friends whether Hindus might find it disrespectful if Dana dressed as a goddess. After all, we didn't want to start a riot or anything. Our friends assured us no one would be offended, but on the way home from the party a strange thing happens. As we are walking down the street to our parked car, an elderly Indian man, dressed only in a checkered lungi, prostrates himself in front of Dana and touches his head to her feet.

Dana looks at me. "Uh, what do I do?"

"Don't ask me," I grumble, still smarting from my contest loss. "You're the goddess."

Dana steeples her hands in front of her in the traditional Indian gesture of greeting known as *namaskar* and solemnly bows her head. The man finally rises and backs away from us, kowtowing all the way. We run giggling to the car, and the man doesn't stop bowing until we are out of sight.

***

While we are sorting out Halloween costumes in Chennai, Sister Theresa is in Hyderabad working on our case for adopting a child. Before we have a chance to tell her we want a girl or perhaps a child with special needs, she tells us a baby is already set aside for us. That is fine with us as we aren't very comfortable with the idea of going to Hyderabad and choosing a child from a lineup. Fortunately, since we live in India we will be able to have foster care of the girl while the case proceeds through the courts, meaning she will live with us a year earlier than she would have otherwise.

By this time I have given Dell notice and am nearing my last day of work and the moment I've been waiting for—letting the nanny go. Although happy to be getting rid of Heather, I dread the prospect of firing another servant. In the end, however, she makes it easy for me to give her the boot.

Shanthi interrupts me one day as I'm speaking to the head of one of India's largest corporations.

"Saar, I need speak with you."

With the phone at my ear, I wave her out of my office and close the door behind her.

She knocks again. "Saar, saar."

I look daggers at her through my office window and drag my finger across my throat. "Yeah, uh-huh," I say to whatever the man has just said to me on the phone.

Shanthi continues knocking. I lock the office door, stretch the phone cord to the bathroom, lock the bathroom door, and sit on the toilet.

Dell India's largest customer wraps up the conversation. "So, then I'll expect to hear from you tomorrow."

"Yeah, absolutely," I reply, wondering what on earth he is talking about. I hang up and go after Shanthi.

"Shanthi, the reason I closed the door is I didn't want to be interrupted."

"Oh, I think you no hear me, saar."

I drop my head into my hands. "But we talked about this before."

"This very, very important, saar."

She informs me, in so many words, that our nanny, Heather, is telling Cole he needs to learn how to properly treat the servants who, by Heather's definition, are inferior. Heather is schooling him in the household hierarchy and how to speak authoritatively to the hired help. Shanthi adds that Heather is stealing from our pantry.

Of course, I realize Shanthi has much to gain by Heather's leaving. First, Leela has been let go, promoting Shanthi from lowly housekeeper to the highly coveted position of cook. If the nanny is out of the house, as well, Shanthi will reign as the undisputed queen of the household. (Dana is, as she suspects, chopped liver.) I listen to Shanthi carefully and then go to the one person I trust completely: Dinesh.

I find him outside detailing the car while Narayanan, the gardener, watches. Without telling him of Shanthi's accusation, I ask Dinesh if he knows anything about someone stealing.

"Yes, saar," he says as if everyone in the world already knows. "Of course."

He takes me behind the servants' quarters and shows me a pile of empty Coca-Cola cans he attributes to Heather's habit of stealing soft drinks from our pantry.

"Heather tells Cole he may not play with Hindu servants. She is not allowing Cole to play with me when saar and madam are not in house, saar."

This makes me very angry. I take a break from work in the afternoon and find Cole in his playroom.

"Why don't you go outside and play with Dinesh?"

"Because, Daddy, you see, Daddy, it's because, you see, well, I can't."

"Why can't you, sweetheart?"

"Because, you see, Heather says he'll make me dirty."

"Make you dirty? How can he make you dirty?"

"Heather, you see, says that if I play with Dinesh, you see…are we going to have a snack? You see, if I play with Dinesh, you see, I'll become dirty like him and Shanthi, you see. So I can't play with them."

"Dinesh and Shanthi aren't dirty, sweetheart. They are wonderful people, and you can play with them anytime you want. Now go outside and play with Dinesh. I'll be there in just a minute."

"Okay, Daddy. I love you, Daddy." He runs off chasing an imaginary friend.

I turn to find Heather standing in the doorway. "I'd like to talk with you outside."

With trepidation, Heather follows me out the door and into the street. I close the solid gate behind us; I'm afraid she might try to upset Cole, who seems vaguely fond of her. Heather vehemently denies everything. She is the victim of an anti-Christian Hindu plot to defame her. She begs, she pleads, and when that doesn't work she gets angry.

"You will pay for this," she hisses through brown teeth.

"I already have. Remember? You still owe me three thousand rupees that I loaned you. Not to mention the Cokes you stole."

With that she knows it's over. "I hate you! I hate you," she screams as I lock her outside.

All the servants except Dinesh, who is in the backyard playing with Cole, have been listening to the entire scene. I don't feel like answering their questions. Instead, I call Dana to tell her what I've done. I worry Cole will be upset to hear Heather's gone, but after I give him the news he never mentions her again. Perhaps he knows she isn't good for him. We run into her on the street six months later, and, happily, he has no recollection of her at all.

Harish invites the family to a friend's beach house for dinner. His friend is a rather endearing odd duck named Simon. Unusually tall and a former policeman, Simon loves American country music most of all. He loves it so much he's built a dance floor just out of reach of high tide and taught one of his hired helpers to DJ. When Simon wants to dance, he throws a little beach sand on the concrete floor and grabs the nearest suitable partner, usually a housekeeper or cook.

Simon plans to develop a beach resort, and toward this end he has erected a dozen or so basic bungalows too far apart and too far from the beach. These bungalows stand in various stages of completion, and it looks as if they haven't been touched in some time. The site lacks landscaping of any kind; ugly weeds grow all around, giving the place the feel of a beachfront ghost town.

During dinner Simon spins fantastic yarns of his cop days and his crazy relatives in the US. On our third and last visit a year and a half later, no further progress has been made on his "resort." Though we try, we never see a bill on any of our visits, and Simon makes us ashamed for even asking.

CHAPTER 21: MR. DAD

I LEAVE DELL SHORTLY BEFORE our new daughter arrives and thus embark on a whole new career. I've fired Heather, the nanny, and am able to spend more time with Cole than since he was born. I love it, and Cole's behavior improves almost immediately. As word circulates among our friends and acquaintances that I've quit my job, I receive the entire gamut of reactions: enthusiasm, surprise, pity, admiration, suspicion, and disgust. Some family members react with disappointment; one is too embarrassed to tell her friends. Others are very supportive. Friends who know me well realize how happy this change will make me; those who don't know me so well are concerned about my decision.

Some friends in the expatriate community whisper about me, while others don't hide their feelings. There is the old slap on the back and "So, I guess you'll be playing a lot of golf then," or "Wow! Are you happy about this?" or the enthusiastic "Greg, I'm so happy for you," or the incredulous "How will you ever get a job again?" There is the hardly veiled contempt of "as a man, I could never do that," or the painful "no way I'm going to let my husband stay home and do nothing." But the most irritating, belittling remark from both friends and family alike is "So, doing the Mr. Mom thing, huh?"

AAAAHHHHH!!!!!! (For advice on what not to say to a male homemaker, check out the excellent piece by Buzz McClain: "Don't Call Me Mr. Mom—What Not to Say to a Stay-at-Home Dad".

Many men think I'm simply nuts and say so, while some women assume I'm a loser. I become a source of humor. One friend simply can't contain her curiosity and asks me the same question one of my lesbian friends got from her boss: "Were you always like this, or is it a new thing?" A Southern Baptist preacher calls our arrangement "unnatural" and "against God's will." A researcher interviews me to test her hypothesis that men who are primary caregivers of children tend toward sexual dysfunction. (See chapter 32 for the answer.) Nevertheless, on the whole, I receive positive reactions from friends and family and many think my decision admirable.

Of course, while the choice to be a full-time homemaker is indeed admirable, I know many of these people find my choice admirable only because I'm a man. Billions of women make the same choice—or don't get a choice at all—and I think few ever call them admirable for it. Women have been doing the same thing since the beginning of time, but I doubt many folks tell them how cool it is they've made the choice to take care of their children full-time.

Don't get me wrong, I appreciate the praise and support, but just don't say it because I'm male. Here's my recommendation: If your mom was a full-time homemaker when you were growing up, get on the phone right now and tell her how admirable and cool that is. And if she worked outside the home, tell her how cool that is too. And then say the same things to your dad while you're at it. Hell, sing "Kumbaya" if you feel like it.

But you're right, I'm cheating. After all, I have a full-time housekeeper *and* cook *and* chauffeur *and* gardener. Being able to afford good people working for me is a luxury most full-time caregivers can only dream of; I can spend all my time focused on my child. I become involved at school, take Cole swimming several times a week, am a regular at the children's library, etc. And at the end of the day, I come home to find the laundry done and a hot dinner on the table. I can give Cole quality time all the time. A full-time job, yes, but one that's a heck of a lot easier than it could've been.

I begin to think Cole's general good behavior means I'm doing a great job or he's an exceptional child, or both. Now, as a parent of three teenagers, I realize that is, for the most part, bullshit. Most children will behave nicely when they have the complete, undivided attention of a doting parent. Wouldn't you? I now know nobody's kids are perfect; they're just kids, and all we can do is give them a strong foundation from which they might make good decisions. And that's a challenge.

Cole and I begin attending a weekly playgroup for children and their mothers. No male has ever been a member of the group, which was begun by the Overseas Women's Club. *Most* members welcome me with open arms, but a few can't accept the idea of a man in a traditionally female role. One mom simply doesn't want me around "spoiling the girl's club."

"Back home I actually knew quite a few Mr. Moms," a young Australian woman says to me on my first day at playgroup. "But you're the first one I've met outside Australia. I'm glad to see it's not just us."

Kristin, who always appears on the verge of a nervous breakdown, remarks, "Greg, you seem to be holding up so well," making me wonder if there is something going on around me of which I'm not aware.

When I host playgroup the first time, someone says, "Greg, your house—it's just so clean."

"Yes, it's very tidy," agrees another.

My house looks just like the others' houses, and, let's face it, none of us actually cleans our own home. I guess they're expecting to find mine to be littered with beer cans and girlie magazines.

I'm shocked to discover that several of the women arrive at playgroup with their nannies in tow. Having a full-time nanny is one thing, but bringing them to playgroup? Get real. Many of my friends take their nannies with them on their vacations so they can lounge at the pool and not play with their kids. I just don't get it, and, thinking I'm among like-minded friends at lunch one day, I make the mistake of opening my mouth and get put in my place rather quickly.

"How can they let some stranger raise their kids when they're not even working?" I ask. "It's just a shame."

This strikes a nerve. "How dare you judge me?" an American friend blurts, red in the face. "I didn't want to come to India. I had a great job back home. If my husband wants me to work, we can leave. Otherwise, I'm going to sit on my ass and enjoy it."

Oh. I hadn't thought of that. Lesson learned: Don't judge.

Truly, life in India has imposed upon many at playgroup an unwelcome state of underemployment since Indian law makes it very difficult for expatriate spouses to work. These restrictions create an anachronistic condition whereby virtually every foreign female in town is a housewife, whether she wants to be or not. In fact, Dana is the only married female I know among the foreign community in Chennai who has a full-time job. Playgroup is full of frustrated doctors, lawyers, nurses, engineers, social workers, and marketing executives who have no possible avenues for their professional ambitions. This is another reason many of them think I'm nuts for quitting my job.

So it is twenty or so women, our kids, and me every Wednesday afternoon, and soon playgroup is the highlight of our social calendar; Cole and I never miss a day. Playgroup's monthly Ladies' Night Out becomes Parents' Night Out, and I'm having more fun than I have since we arrived in Chennai. Theoretically, husbands are now welcome at Parents' Nights Out, but I'm the only male who comes. This event allows me to learn a lot about women. For example, although I had suspicions, I wasn't entirely sure that women were as obsessed with sex as men. Well, now I know they are more so. It's all they talk about. I think I can handle anything they throw at me, but when they discuss the proper use of Ben Wa balls, I can't help but blush.

I try to arrange playdates with friends from playgroup and right away learn who's open to the idea of hanging out with a man and his kids and who considers the idea absurd. I make several good friends and learn a lot about parenting. After a while there are four or five women with whom I spend most of my time. I also try to get together with a consulate mother, Susan, who has two girls, ages five and two.

"Why don't y'all come over for a while?" I ask. "Cole would really like to see Sedona, and Shanthi's going to make some fried cheese."

Susan covers the receiver with her hand and engages in a protracted negotiation with her four-year-old, who clearly has the upper hand.

"I'm sorry, Greg. Sedona doesn't want to go right now," she whines. "She says she'd like to watch TV."

After this happens a few more times, I make up my mind to concentrate on friends who don't live by the whims of their preschool-aged children. Then one day Susan calls and invites us over to play. I load Cole in the car and head over, excited at the prospect of some adult conversation. She meets us at the door looking pained.

"I'm so sorry, but we'll have to cancel. Sedona says she doesn't want to share her toys today. You understand, don't you?"

"Why didn't her mama just tell her she has to share her toys," Cole asks as we drive away.

"Beats me, Son. Beats me."

Though I'm adjusting well to my new job, Dana convinces me to sign up for the Foreign Service exam again just to keep my options open. After having failed the exam for a *second time*, stupid pride makes me reluctant to try again since I already know I will make the best Foreign Service officer ever in the history of the world. I take and pass the written exam again and register to take the oral component for the third time later in the year.

✺✺✺

Working for Dell was lucrative and somewhat exciting, but at the end of the day, I wasn't doing anything to save the world—my ultimate goal—or even improve the lives of those around me. Just after I leave Dell, I decide to find myself some humanitarian work I can do while Cole is at school. In the past I had always been able to provide many plausible excuses for having no time to volunteer. Now I have none, and so I'm ready to put my time where my mouth is. I settle on a combination home for the destitute elderly and day-care center for children of single mothers run by a group of nuns on the south side of town. ("What do children of single fathers do?" I wonder.)

My foreign presence at the home creates quite a stir. I tell the good nuns I'll do any job to help. They give me tea.

"Come tomorrow, and we'll find some work for you," they say.

The next day I'm again given tea—and the next day—and the next. On the fifth day I turn down the tea and go looking for work.

Dozens of metal bunks with dingy mattresses are arranged in rows in a large open-air bungalow. Some of the bunks are occupied, but most are not. One bedridden man tells me most residents are exercising, and I help a staff member strip the sheets off the beds. Every day until noon I go there and find something to clean or repair, and soon Dinesh begins helping as well. I perform the symbolically important task of cleaning the bathrooms, and this strategy works; the nuns begin to take me seriously.

The home houses about two hundred men and women, most of whom are quite advanced in age. They have nowhere to go and would be on the street if not for the nuns, who give them a bunk and three meals a day. They are eager to talk with me.

"We come from all walks of life and various castes, but everybody is equal here," a retired librarian tells me.

In an isolated corner of the compound, three men and one woman live in what can only be described as cages. One of the men is chained to the wall; he lunges at me repeatedly until I leave the area. The woman is nude.

"These people are violent and cannot live in society," a nun tells me. "They were abandoned by their families long ago. The government will not care for them. We keep them here so they can do no harm to themselves and others."

I soon leave, driven silently by Dinesh, thinking about this. I wonder if, given the proper resources, those folks could get better and not have to live in such conditions. On the way home we drive by the municipal water complex, where tankers are filled to deliver water to the neighborhood cisterns of the poor and to the private cisterns of the wealthy. Since filling these trucks is a leaky business, a great amount of water rushes along the curb, picking up filth and dirt. Just after this stream passes under the chain-link fence surrounding the compound, a large number of women corral the water with their feet or a rag and wash their clothes in the putrid pools that form. This seems to me an act of terrible desperation, and I remark to Dinesh how randomly good fortune has been doled out.

"It's just not fair."

"Yes, saar. It is true, saar. But this water is cleaner than Adyar River's water, saar."

"Yes, I suppose so. I didn't think about that."

On subsequent visits to the home, the residents often thank me and Dinesh as we are going about our work.

"You don't need to thank me," I tell them. "It's my pleasure to be here." I'm not lying. I knew my service would help others, but I didn't quite understand how good it could be for *me*.

CHAPTER 22: WHAT CHILD IS THIS?

November 13, 2000

THE BABY GIRL DESTINED FOR us is an eight-month-old named Theekshana (no last name). On Cole's fourth birthday we receive our first picture of her. A cute butterball of a baby frowns at us from an orange chair, and we are excited to learn we may have foster care of her as early as Christmas. We later learn that Theekshana was very thin when she got to the orphanage, but by the time the picture was taken she'd porked up rather nicely under Sister Theresa's care.

We learn that Theekshana is almost certainly a member of an ethnic group called the Lambada. (No relation to the Latin American song and dance of the same name.) These people live almost exclusively in the Indian state of Andhra Pradesh and are officially designated a "backward caste" by the Indian government, which explains the way Theekshana crawls—backward. The only evidence we have of her biological parents is two fingerprints on a relinquishment document that was read to them, since they could neither read nor write.

Officially, she was relinquished because of medical problems her family could not afford to treat. She reportedly had several sisters and was born around a certain festival day. Sister Theresa tells us Theekshana's parents were itinerant construction workers—just like the community of people living and working on the construction site next door to The Flame. The orphanage set her birthday in late March.

I begin preparing Cole for what will certainly be the single most earth-shattering event in his short life to date. He is excited at the idea of having a new sister to play with, even though I explain what the presence of a sibling will mean in terms of sharing toys and attention. I realize now that trying to prepare a child for the arrival of a sibling is like trying to prepare your wife for an upcoming extramarital affair.

A few days after we receive Theekshana's picture, Sister Theresa calls us very early in the morning.

"Everything is in order. Please come and pick up Theekshana."

"Oh. OK. But I thought she wouldn't come live with us until after Christmas."

"God has different plans."

Needless to say, all hell breaks loose. I assemble the staff and have them go through boxes of stored items looking for baby clothes. I call friends to borrow a crib. We decide I will fly to Hyderabad for Theekshana in the morning while Dana and Cole go on an emergency shopping spree.

I'm more than a little nervous. Cole is a big boy now; have I forgotten how to handle a baby? What if Theekshana cries all the way home because we're strangers? What if she doesn't like me? People will stare. They'll be thinking, "Poor guy, he doesn't have any idea what he's doing." Perhaps I'm being paranoid. Perhaps not: The orphanage staff is quite alarmed when I arrive alone.

"Please come back with good sir's wife or good sir's nanny," they say.

"I'm perfectly capable of taking care of Theekshana on the way home."

"A baby is needing a woman's touch, sir."

I begin to get irritated.

Sister Theresa intervenes. "Let them go! Let them go! God is watching over them."

I give Theekshana one last look around the orphanage before Sister Theresa escorts us to the airport in an old Ambassador. There are no seat belts in the vehicle, let alone a car seat. Theekshana sits between us, happy as a clam, with no idea of what's in store for her or all that she is leaving behind. I'm wondering how it's possible that there was a time in my own country when we simply put children in the car and let them climb around wherever they wanted. I remember Great-Aunt Birdie holding the steering wheel and a Pall

Mall in one hand while with the other she enforced order between my brother and me in the back seat.

We get to the airport in one piece, and Sister Theresa says goodbye to us at the curb. I'm the only one who's sad when we part; the good sister has done this too many times, and Theekshana doesn't understand and won't remember. By the time we get back to Hyderabad to visit the orphanage someday, the nun will almost certainly not be around. (Read the epilogue.) I bid an emotional farewell to her on Theekshana's behalf. Sister Theresa is then driven away, leaving me and Theekshana standing on the curb in front of the airport with all of India staring at us.

I have been with Cole since day one. I know all his likes and habits and can identify his cry in a room crowded with children. I can still tell what he needs practically before he needs it. We are in sync. I know nothing, however, about this pudgy child in my arms. How does she like to be held? How does she cry when she's hungry? How does she like to be comforted?

We check in for our flight. So far, so good. Flying on Jet Airways, I know the plane will not likely be delayed. Air India and Indian Airlines always are delayed due to maintenance problems. Jet Airways, with much newer planes, never seems to have these issues. Since regional airports in India have relatively little traffic, there are almost never delays due to air-traffic congestion. I feel confident the plane will leave on time. We proceed to the gate and have a seat, and almost immediately there is an announcement.

"Ladies and gentlemen, due to an unexpected late arrival of the aircraft from New Delhi, Flight 189 to Chennai will be delayed approximately one hour."

Indian airports are not exactly set up for parents traveling with infants. In this particular airport not only are there no baby-changing tables in the bathrooms, there are also no paper towels, toilet paper, stall doors, toilet seats, or running water. Theekshana begins to get fussy. I begin to sweat. I have enough baby formula to last us a week, but I need to find some bottled water to mix it with.

Uh-oh, Code Brown, big-time. After a quick look in the bathroom, I opt to lay Theekshana across a chair and change her. Impatient travelers now pack the waiting room. I love Indian people. I really do. But I must say that, in general, they have absolutely no qualms about getting into someone else's business. I realize I'm being watched. A woman makes a beeline for me from across the departure lounge.

"Why don't you change her diaper in the bathroom?" She harrumphs.

For the record, I don't say, "Why don't you sit your butt down and mind your own business?" Instead, I reply, "I'm sorry. The men's bathroom is too disgusting."

"This is disgraceful." She snarls. "Changing a girl baby in public."

"And what would you like me to do, madam?" I'm finished by now, but the woman lingers to chastise me.

"You should be ashamed. Where is this child's mother?"

I pick up Theekshana and hit the road. We walk the airport from top to bottom. My arms are really tired, but I'm not about to let Theekshana scoot around on the dirty floor. I strap her on my front in a baby carrier, and she seems to like that. Finally, we are about to board. I had hoped my walking would put Theekshana to sleep, but she remains wide awake and ready to party. As I pace the waiting area, two young female flight attendants approach me.

"Sir, is this your baby?"

As I mentioned, Theekshana is strapped to my chest.

"What baby?"

They don't laugh. "We think you need to remove your baby from—that *thing*."

"Oh, yes. I will certainly take her out before takeoff, if that's what you mean."

"No sir. You need to take her out now," the young lady persists.

"And why is that?" Do they suspect the ol' bomb-in-the-diaper trick?

"She must be uncomfortable in that. Why don't you just hold her?"

"Y'all don't get out much, do you? Many people use these in my country."

"Sir, is your wife with you? Could we speak to her?"

I've had enough. Fortunately for these young women, a voice announces our flight will board, and, for the second time in an hour, I turn my back on a complete stranger. Every able person storms the gate.

To generalize again, Indians, as a people, tend to have difficulty waiting in line. Or, let's say, they wait in line differently. People will push, shove, and be quite rude even when there is clearly nothing to be gained by such behavior, a tactic entirely out of character with most Indians' kind, hospitable demeanor. You can witness this phenomenon in the US in an airport that is boarding a direct flight to India. Utter mayhem. In New York, I once saw frustrated airline personnel refuse to board a flight to New Delhi until everybody sat down and shut up.

Theekshana and I finally board and sit next to a foreign man with a long beard and dreadlocks. He is wearing sunglasses and a Hawaiian-print shirt open to his navel. India is full of Americans and Europeans who have come here to drop out of Western society. They move to places like Goa and live in huts on the beach and stop wearing shirts. They have been known to sell drugs, open dusty bars with names like "Titties," or operate popular grunge-backpacker guesthouses that frequently are infested with bedbugs. Sometimes these people are a lot of fun. Not this guy.

Not only does he take up the whole armrest, his arm is actually two or three inches on our side. Theekshana and I are sharing a seat, and we need the room.

"Hi. Would you mind moving your arm a bit?"

"No!"

Fine. It isn't worth arguing over. The guy ignores the instructions of a flight attendant and whips out a laptop before we leave the ground. He examines the device from every angle as if he has never seen it before. I watch him from the corner of my eye while he figures out how to open the screen latch. He experiments with the pressing of keys and mouse clicks.

Theekshana has fallen asleep on me by this time, and I continue to watch his attempts to use various software programs. He examines with great ardor every pocket of the computer's carrying bag, clearly surprised at what he finds there. Eventually, I get bored and tune out.

As the flight drones on, the man annexes more and more of our seat with his arm.

"Could you move your arm, please?"

"Shut up."

When we begin our descent, the change in air pressure starts Theekshana crying. As there is not a lot I can do about this, I place her head on my shoulder nearest my neighbor and let her get her cry out. It feels good for both of us.

"Can't you get that kid to be quiet?"

"Shut up," I reply with a smile.

We finally disembark on the tarmac in Chennai, and I stop one of several security personnel.

"If anyone reported a laptop stolen, I know who did it," I say and point to our neighbor on the plane.

When we enter the building, the foreign man is on the tarmac inside a circle of radio-wielding airport officials and police.

Since we don't have any checked luggage, Theekshana and I leave the airport ahead of our fellow passengers. What a day! I can't wait to get to the safety and quiet of our car. I clutch Theekshana closely as we walk the gauntlet of hopeful taxi drivers, baggage handlers, beggars, and touts, looking for our familiar red Jeep. Dinesh, Dana, and Cole are nowhere in sight. I had called Dana on my mobile phone just before we got on the plane, so she knew exactly when we would arrive. We stand in the middle of this chaos searching in vain until a policeman snarls at us to move along so others can exit.

We aren't allowed back in the airport, so I move away from the exit as much as I can without being run over in the street. I call Dana. No answer. We wait. Theekshana begins to cry. Sweat is dripping into my eyes.

Half an hour later, I'm so angry you could have fried eggs on my forehead. Just as I plan to give up and take a taxi, Dana, Cole, and Dinesh roll up, grinning broadly. Instead of a happy arrival for our new baby in Chennai, she gets to listen her new daddy vent his accumulated steam from the stressful day. Dana ignores me as best she can, Cole cries at seeing me so upset, and Dinesh doesn't say a word.

Finally, I am spent, and we finish the ride in silence. When we get home, the servants go nuts over Theekshana, and I collapse on the couch. After a few beers, my troubles are forgotten—almost.

❄❄❄

Theekshana's cute picture hasn't done her justice, and we are thrilled she sleeps through the night right away. Curiously, she doesn't cry much; Dana falls asleep one Saturday during Theekshana's afternoon nap and wakes up a few hours later to find her awake in her crib and waiting quietly. I guess that comes from growing up in an orphanage.

At this point, we have a beautiful baby in our custody, and we haven't signed a single paper or been visited by a social worker. The lack of oversight is disconcerting.

I call Sister Theresa to ask. "Shouldn't we do some paperwork or something?"

"Not to worry," she assures me. "This can be taken care of later."

We are told the entire adoption will be legal in a month, and, with that, it seems we will enjoy the world's fastest adoption. In reality, we will tread a long, painful path before Theekshana is legally a member of our family.

A month or so after Theekshana arrives a social worker visits to complete a home study. We spend fifteen minutes over tea answering a few questions about ourselves. We eventually come to the question of employment.

"I see on your application that your wife works at the American Consulate and that you, Mr. Buford, are a homemaker. Obviously, the professions have been switched. I'll just correct this document now."

"No, actually, that is correct."

"You are a homemaker?"

"That's right."

"Are you looking for a job?"

"No."

"I don't understand. Who will support this child?"

"My wife works at the American Consulate," I say, getting anxious.

"Then who will take care of this child during the day?"

"I will."

She scribbles furiously on her papers. "You will have a nanny then?"

"Nope. I just left a well-paid job in order to take care of my two children. I don't want a nanny."

"Mr. Buford, do you do any work at all? This is very strange."

"As I have said, my job is taking care of my children. That is what I do."

Writing ever more furiously, she says, "I mean, do you have any paid job?"

I'm formulating a response that likely would have gotten us in trouble, when Dana comes to the rescue.

"Greg is a writer. In fact, he is working on a book about our life in India."

"Oh, I see."

Obviously relieved, the social worker stops writing and soon leaves with a smile. Only several months later do Dana and I see the completed home study, long after it has been submitted in quintuplicate to the appropriate government ministry. We don't recognize the folks described within. The document describes both of us in erroneous detail as if the social worker had simply made it up.

We supply reams of documents to the adoption court, most of which have to be on special paper. We must purchase paper embossed with twenty-rupee or one hundred-rupee revenue stamps and print on them whatever information the court requires. In many countries that don't have well-developed methods for collecting sales or income taxes, this is a common method of generating government revenue. Incidentally, these are the same type of stamps that the British Parliament forced American colonists to purchase, leading to cries of "no taxation without representation" and ultimately to war.

Theekshana is a child of mystery. Her legal birthdate is March 23, but we suspect she is younger. The consulate doctor, Dr. John, believes she is a healthy five-month-old. The orphanage insists Theekshana had been approximately three weeks old when her biological parents relinquished her and that she had been with the orphanage for seven months. When we press Sister Theresa for proof of this, she mistakenly sends us documents concerning a different child. Dr. John insists Theekshana can't possibly be her legal age unless she had been born quite premature, in which case she would likely not have survived more than a few days in rural India. We will probably never know for sure. We like her anyway.

Theekshana has one distinguishing mark on her body that causes us some concern: a very large and messy scar on her left wrist. Dr. John ventures it might be the result of a sloppy intravenous injection, but he considers that unlikely since she probably wouldn't have had access to such medical care in her village. Sister Theresa claims Theekshana had been given no intravenous medication while at the orphanage, and she doesn't remember her having any scar. It is possible, Dr. John tells us, the scar is the result of an attempt by someone to end Theekshana's life before she was taken to the orphanage. Another thing about Theekshana we will never know for sure.

Theekshana has beautiful brown skin that is somewhat lighter than typical of South Indians, and her eyes are teardrop-shaped, unlike those of most Indians whom anthropologists classify, generally, as Caucasian and who tend to have round eyes like people of European descent. Theekshana's eyes evoke thoughts of people living farther east. Their color is a brown so dark it approaches black, and thin black hair crowns her chubby body. Initially a very quiet baby, Theekshana seems a little confused but not put out by her new surroundings. I watch her sleep with her thumb in her mouth and wonder about her past. There are so many things I would like to know about her, if only she could tell me.

"It's too bad that Nina is Indian," Cole says to me with a sad look on his face.

I'm duly alarmed. "Why do you say that?"

"Because when she grows up, we won't be able to talk with her."

"You are really confusing me. Why won't we be able to talk with her?"

"Because she'll speak Telugu"—the principal language of the state of Andhra Pradesh—"and we only know English."

"Hmm. That could be a problem. We'll just have to wait and see."

Cole is initially upset that Theekshana is an infant. He naturally assumed his new sister would be an instant playmate for him since I had neglected to mention she wouldn't even be walking yet. After this initial disappointment, Cole bounces around her in circles like a puppy for the first month before the honeymoon ends. Overall, he takes the shock of having a sibling fairly well, and I do everything I can to make him a part of the time I need to spend with Theekshana. This stretches me pretty thin.

I go back to the old folks' home and explain to the nuns that I need to take care of my own for the time being. I'm sure I live up to their expectation of a rich foreigner who would stop volunteering when the novelty wore off. I promise myself I'll make it up to the world someday.

✲✲✲

Eventually, we decide "Theekshana" is too difficult for our redneck relatives to pronounce, and so we decide to name our new daughter Nina Theekshana. Nina is an Indian name that means "beautiful eyes" in Sanskrit, the "Latin of India." *Nina* has the added value of being easy to say by almost anyone in the world. Before we come up with Nina, however, Theekshana remains for weeks without a permanent first name while we dither over what to call her. Each morning Dana's consular section colleagues sift through the day's visa applications, shouting out interesting names to the room for an instant poll. Here are some of the names that didn't make it:

Tamali—a great name meaning "dark bark," but I get homesick for Mexican food every time I hear it.

Shilpa—the local staff in Dana's office picks this name. Try to say "Cole! Shilpa! Be quiet and eat your supper!" It just doesn't work.

Wumika—a beautiful name, which in ancient Sanskrit literally means "sounds really nice especially when you tack 'Buford' on the end of it."

Vijayalakshmikamalaanjupremakalavishnutoyotaharikrishnanj ayalalithaa—we like the way this one sounds but turn it down because it's much too common in South India.

S PEAKING OF NAMES, MINE HAS changed since I left my job. The
consulate has always known me as a result of my relationship
with Dana, and often I'm referred to as "Mr. Williams," particularly
by the local staff, who are unaccustomed to finding married
foreigners with different surnames. While I still had a paying job I
could be Greg Buford—at least while at Dell HQ in Bangalore—but
I don't even have that anymore.

Soon after I leave Dell, I just can't be bothered correcting
people, and I'm more often than not called incorrectly. Although I
don't mind being called by my wife's name, I pity the fool who dares
call Dana "Mrs. Buford," which makes her crazy. Naturally, I use
her disdain for being identified by my last name to drive her nuts,
calling her simply "Wife of Greg Buford" if she really gets out of
line. But whatever you want to call her, Wife of Greg Buford (WGB)
surprises everyone when she single-handedly crushes a major
immigrant smuggling operation!

Dana's job as vice-consul at the American Consulate in Chennai
means she spends the greater part of each day interviewing visa
applicants. On a typical day she sees many fraudulent documents,
and her office constantly tries to discover patterns of fraud. One
week, Dana notices a rash of people coming to her window fitting
the following profile: a newly married couple seeks tourist visas,

husband does all the talking, wife speaks only a local language (in other words, not English, like many educated Indians), husband is young and well dressed, wife is not so young and looks thoroughly out of place in her fancy clothes. When Dana interviews yet another couple fitting this profile, unerring instincts tell her something is amiss.

She separates the couple and questions each of them about their married life together. When the stories don't match, she allows the woman to leave—a clear sign of (sadly, justified) anti-male bias on Dana's part—and proceeds to tighten the screws on the "husband." (Not literally; at that time the State Department did not sanction that sort of thing.) He refuses at first to crack under Dana's intense questioning, so she wonders aloud if she should get the Indian police involved. (Unbeknownst to the suspect, the Indian police would most certainly have done nothing.) He begins to sweat.

At this point, the fact that the man doesn't simply call her bluff is telling, because the rich and well connected have absolutely no fear of the Indian police. Dana orders him to wait in the detention room—known during happier hours as the lunch room—until she can decide what to do with him. She has, actually, no authority whatsoever to hold this man, and he could leave at any point. The worst she can do is make him permanently ineligible for a US visa. He doesn't, however, know that, and so she leaves him there to stew and goes out for a *thali*. A thali is the Indian equivalent of the *prix fixe* or *comida corrida* lunch, a set meal of several dishes that changes daily and, typically, is all-you-can-eat. It is undoubtedly the best way to eat Indian food.

After a long lunch—moong dal, cauliflower with turmeric and fennel, eggplant *bartha*, sour soup-like *sambar*, curd, rice, chapatti—Dana summons the man to her office.

"Tell the truth now," she says in the same voice she uses when Cole throws food on the floor. "We know you are involved in an international immigrant smuggling ring, so you may as well confess!" And guess what: He confesses! WGB is a hero! We never learn exactly why this man is trying to get this woman to the US, but the previous year Chennai had been the base of operations for a group smuggling women to San Francisco to work as prostitutes. Dana is commended for her vigilance, and the consulate is put on alert.

✻✻✻

Fresh from Dana's victory over organized crime, we go to the annual charity Christmas party organized by the International Women's Association. The IWA doesn't know how to deal with me. There is talk of creating a men's auxiliary. They contemplate making me an "honorary woman" in order to formally include me in their membership. I decline this gracious offer. I ask them to change the exclusive nature of their organization by calling it the International Spouses' Association and allowing me to join as a man. Well, that doesn't fly, but it doesn't stop us from going to their parties, which are often the best Chennai has to offer.

At the Christmas party, I meet many of my playgroup friends' husbands for the first time. Alcatel has a large design laboratory in Chennai, and the entire expatriate staff is men, mostly Belgians. Virtually all of their wives attend playgroup along with Cole, Nina, and me, and several of the Belgian women hang out with me on a regular basis outside of the group. Many of them have children in Cole's prekindergarten class, and we attend many of the same parties. Their husbands don't have much use for someone like me.

"I've heard about you," one of them says in a derisive tone.

"Oh, really? What did they tell you?" I ask, but his eyes have already drifted away.

"How can you let your wife make more than you?" asks another.

Before I can answer, my friend Peggy's husband, Pieter, asks, "So you're the guy who is with our wives while we're at work?"

"That's right. I know all their secrets."

We leave as they begin to tell off-color jokes about Blacks, Jews, Indians, etc.

Much has been made of Americans' ugliness abroad and our lack of cultural sensitivity. Yet in Chennai I've met many foreigners, mostly Continental Europeans, who don't associate with Indians at all and turn up their noses at the very idea of eating Indian food. They live years in India without making an Indian friend or venturing beyond the doors of the international chain hotels that serve milkshakes, hamburgers, and sushi. Not saying we don't have our share of bigotry; we just don't have a monopoly.

✳✳✳

After I fire Heather, the nanny, and Leela, the cook, Shanthi takes over kitchen duties in addition to her housekeeping duties, and she occasionally watches over Cole and Nina when I have an errand. This makes for a pretty hard day for her. She never complains—well, some—but when I find my favorite blue shirt ironed and folded in the refrigerator, I know it's time to get her some help.

"Shanthi, do you know someone who needs a part-time job?"

"I am knowing one girl, saar."

"And you can get along with her?"

"I am not understanding, saar."

"I mean, are you going to fight with her?"

Shanthi laughs aloud at the notion. "No, of course, saar. I am not fighting with anyone!"

Kutti arrives at our door within the hour. An Indian woman once told my wife, Dana, that she is too thin to ever look right in a sari.

Looking at Kutti, I now understand what she meant. Anyway, time to conduct an interview.

"Have a seat, Kutti."

Kutti remains standing. Shanthi takes a seat. "I will stay here, saar."

"Whatever. Kutti, do you have any experience?"

Kutti blinks at me in silence.

"Do you speak any English, Kutti?"

"Kutti is speaking English very well, saar," Shanthi interjects, "and she is cleaning for Singapore's family long time."

"OK. On what days are you able to work, Kutti?"

Kutti stares at me with a lost look on her face, her mouth hanging open. She needs dental work to correct a terrible overbite.

"If anything you want saying to Kutti, you talking to me, OK," Shanthi says. "Kutti is no talking to you."

"Fair enough," I say, having gotten used to things like this. "I'll talk to you, Shanthi, when I want to talk to Kutti."

"Yes, saar."

I ask several more questions, to which Shanthi responds while Kutti nods in shy agreement.

"Shanthi, how do you know the answers to all these questions I am asking Kutti?"

"Kutti is my younger *sister*, saar. You don't know? She is looking like me, saar!"

I consider the two of them. Shanthi is tall and busty with ample child-bearing hips. Their other sister, Selvi, who worked for us briefly when we first arrived in India, is short and overweight. Kutti looks like a broomstick wrapped in a sari, and I see no family resemblance whatsoever.

"Only Kutti is very thin, saar."

"Yes, I can see that. Did you and Selvi let her have anything to eat when she was little?"

"No, saar," Shanthi replies with dead seriousness.

I rub my eyes. "Sorry. That was supposed to be a joke."

"Ha," Shanthi cries, punching me on the arm. "I am joking, saar! Of course, we give her food, saar."

I laugh. "Yep. You got me. Fine. She's hired."

I find it isn't necessary to say much to Kutti, because she does her work and she doesn't ask me to solve her personal crises. And as every manager knows, a quiet employee is a good employee. I rarely find her lounging except when she and Shanthi take their two-hour afternoon nap under our dining room table. I come to find the sound of their synchronous snoring strangely soothing.

Kutti has great fear of me; she leaves any room when I enter and not slowly. She drops her broom and flees, bangles jingling. I suppress the urge to give her a big hug and tell her everything's going to be OK, mainly because she would drop dead on the spot. Kutti never engages the children in any way. After she has been working for us for some months, Cole asks, "Who is that other woman in the kitchen with Shanthi?" Kutti is just a ghost in our house, and we leave her alone to do her work.

I suspect Kutti is disabled in some way. "Why does Kutti not speak? Why is she so afraid?" I ask Shanthi on a lazy afternoon.

"Kutti is working very hard," she responds with finality, to which I can't disagree.

CHAPTER 24: STILL NAVY AFTER ALL THESE YEARS

MY MOTHER- AND FATHER-IN-LAW COME to see us. Although they have both been out of a job for more than a year, they live on a permanent spending spree and don't think twice about plunking down a few thousand bucks to spend ten days with us in India. Must be nice. We are happy to have them because they love the kids, they are curious about India, and they like to do stuff. We proudly show them around Chennai like city boosters, explaining India to them as if we are natives, having, after all, now been in the country an entire year, our halfway point. We take them to our favorite restaurants, interpret Indian English for them, and introduce them to our, now numerous, Indian friends, who win them over immediately with their grace and hospitality.

"It looks like y'all are really enjoying it here," my mother-in-law, Kay, observes.

Hmm. Interesting. India's rough. I mean, for folks who grew up with the advantages, luxuries, and expectations of an upper-middle-income American household, India presents its challenges and deprivations. I've listed many in this book. Some of the consulate Americans can't handle the stress; they freak out and leave. Not infrequently, we are faced with frustrating situations. For example, we encounter the local caddy mafia when Dana decides to take up golf. (Keep an eye on your clubs!) I have to remind myself that I can choose to laugh about it, cry about it, or get angry. The best choice is to laugh. *Always*.

But, at the end of the day, India has one redeeming asset, one thing above all that saves us and keeps us coming back for more, and that is *its people*, caddies notwithstanding. Without our Indian friends our success is not assured, and we've noticed that the foreigners among us who enjoy India the most are the ones who let down their guard and allow themselves to make local friends. We are, indeed, making it in India and managing to enjoy ourselves. Surely our sponsor, Nancy, would have a term to describe this phase of our relationship with India, but she has moved on to another country of assignment, and Dana and I are now sponsoring consulate newbies, the old India hands that we are.

We take Kay and Terry with us to Rani's, a furniture factory and wholesaler located in a series of decrepit mansions near the city center. The heart of the place is a colonial-era manor house, every room stacked to the ceiling with antique teak and rosewood furniture. Dana and I intend to buy a few pieces of Rani's furniture before leaving India. I mention to my in-laws that, judging by the popularity of Rani's goods among the expatriate community, a decent living could be made importing such furniture for sale in the US. As usual, Terry and Kay don't seem to pay much attention to what I say, but soon they talk of giving up their job searches—he is an electrical engineer and she an educator—and going into the furniture business. Dana and I only laugh and figure a trip to Pondicherry will be right up their alley.

Many Americans are aware that India was once a British colony. Far fewer realize that other nations had their pieces of India and that the Brits were simply the most successful of India's Western invaders. The French had several small enclaves in India, including Pondicherry, which they took in 1674. The Portuguese also had their territories, the most famous being Goa, while the Dutch and the Danes preferred trade to empire-building, at least in India. Only in 1947 did the French return Pondicherry to the Indians, and it retains vestiges of colonial rule.

Many buildings in the city center are decidedly French in style, including the Hotel de Ville and the French Consulate. Walking through the few square blocks of French colonial homes, complete with plantation shutters and door placards in French, you can almost forget for a moment that you are in India. Almost. At any rate, it's a relaxing place to go when the hustle and bustle of modern India becomes too much and you need something besides Indian food for a few days. Proof of French influence can be found in the local cuisine, at least in the historic district, and we enjoy passable beef bourguignon and fresh baguettes on our visit.

Visitors also go to Pondy to rummage through the quaint antique shops lining the narrow streets of the French Quarter. By the time we get there, my in-laws are in the furniture business "hook, line, and sinker," and they salivate over the deals to be had. The furniture import kick has gotten out of hand, and they hardly talk about anything else for the rest of the trip.

Sure enough, when they get back to Texas they import several containers of furniture, rent warehouse space, buy a giant delivery truck—which, much to the chagrin of their neighbors, they park in the driveway of their upscale Austin home—and begin travelling the country selling Indian furniture at flea markets and such. They don't make much money at it, but they really love what they are doing. Who would've thought?

Soon after Terry and Kay leave, we get word that a US Navy ship will dock in Chennai for the first time in many years. An official reception is to be held on the destroyer, the USS Something-or-Other, with all the right Indians in attendance, and this requires Dana's presence in her official capacity as American diplomat. Spouses are invited as well, which means I, more or less, have to go. That's OK because I'm getting bored with the same tired restaurants and nightspots, and I've never been on a working ship before.

We play the good diplomats, introducing local Indian dignitaries—we know many of them from the fancy-pants parties we attend—to the Navy officers, who give us a tour of their boat. Protocol dictates that only after the departure of official guests and the most senior diplomat present—the consul general—are junior officers like Dana allowed to leave. Luckily, the bigwigs make a short night of it, and we get off the hook early.

Several young sailors ask me to be their tour guide for a night on the town. Dana gives me her blessing and goes home to bed. Five young men hoot and holler as they run below decks to change out of their dress uniforms, emerging several minutes later looking more like the kids they are in their blue jeans and T-shirts.

I approach two auto-rickshaw drivers waiting on the pier and begin to negotiate a price.

The sailors climb in the vehicles ahead of me. "Go! Just go," they shout, and we take off with them shouting profanities at passing cars for kicks.

Since good bars are hard to find in Chennai outside of private clubs and fancy hotels, I direct our drivers to a social club owned by some friends, the Patels, which occupies the top two floors of a very desirable building. On the lower floor is an exercise gym and pool hall; Chinese, Indian, and Continental restaurants are on the top. The Continental restaurant sits on a terrace overlooking the city. The food is Indianized but very reasonable. The Patels have made Dana and me honorary club members, and we visit frequently because there is a good playroom with an attendant for the kids.

Upon arriving at the club, the sailors won't pay for the ride because the auto-rickshaw drivers had refused to let them hang on the outside of their vehicles. I pay the tab while the sailors harass the bouncer barring their entry to the building. The guard recognizes me and admits us with the sailors promising to "come back and kick your ass later." On our way up, my new friends make lewd propositions to the hapless young elevator operator.

"Y'all need to tone it down," I say.

"Tone it down? What the #$%@?"

Getting off the elevator, these fine representatives of our nation's military ignore the man asking for their membership cards and demand to know if they're in the "playaz" club. I apologize to the attendant, tell him my name, and lead the sailors to the bar, where I think they will do the least amount of damage.

"Boy, get us some booze," one of the sailors shouts at the tuxedoed bartender.

"All right. That's enough," I say.

Two young Indian women at a nearby table turn and stare at us.

A sailor points at them. "Oh my goodness, ladies! Who let the dogs out?"

The comedian's comrades-in-arms bark like dogs at these two women, who beat a wise and hasty retreat.

"Hey, Bartender. We told you to get us something to drink! What the @#$%^ is wrong with you?"

"If y'all don't calm down, they're going to kick us out," I say to them.

"Let those @#$%^& Indians try it. We'll kick their asses!"

And things basically go downhill from there. They relieve the bartender of a bottle of tequila and pass it around. It's my turn. I begin to feel very old.

"Uh, no thanks."

I find Sanjay Patel in the lobby berating his security guards for having let the sailors in. He immediately drops what he is doing and greets me warmly.

"Greg, it's so good to see you. I hope Dana and the kids are well. Listen, I'm terribly sorry. I just have to take care of a minor crisis, and then I'll come talk with you. It seems some interlopers have entered the club."

"No, I'm the one who's sorry. I'm afraid those idiots are with me. I'll pay for everything." I explain the story. "I never should've brought them here."

"Not to worry, Greg. But there is a man downstairs who refuses to leave because your friends broke the canopy of his auto-rickshaw."

There is a crash of breaking glass behind me.

"Wait here. I'll handle this." I race back to the bar.

"And you don't have to call me darlin', darlin'," the sailors sing, arms around shoulders.

I decide I'll throw them out myself or die trying rather than make my Indian friend do it.

"Gentlemen," I roar, "it's time to go."

"What time is it?" one drunken sailor slurs. "We have to be back on ship at midnight."

It is 9:15.

"I don't know, man. I left my @#$%^ watch on the #$%^& ship," yells another.

"My watch is still on Hong Kong time," laments a third.

The others don't seem to be able to tell time at all at this point. (This was a time before mobile phones traveled well.)

"Holy @#$%^," I yell. "It's fifteen till twelve. Quick, let's get you out of here!"

The sailors conga-line behind me to the lobby, where I order the terrified elevator operator to get off and let me drive. I sigh in relief when the door closes on us.

"Man, you guys are going to be in big trouble if you don't make it back in time."

I herd them out of the building past the bouncer they earlier threatened and into a couple of auto-rickshaws. I pay for the torn canopy.

"Where to take them, saar?"

"I don't care; just don't bring them back here," I say, handing the drivers a fistful of rupees and waving them off.

The sailors roar off into the humid Chennai night. "Later, dude!"

I never know if they make it back to the ship in time—or ever—and, frankly, I don't care. I head back upstairs to apologize to Sanjay and pay for the damage but am instead treated to a late dinner. We remain there together, eating and laughing, looking down on the city below, into the early morning.

CHAPTER 25: LOAN RANGER

W E PAY OUR SERVANTS A living wage—high by local standards—yet they have perennial cash-flow issues. In our experience, Indians of relatively low economic means often live with large extended families in close quarters, and for every family member with a decent job, there may be several more out of work and living off the one earner's wages. We learn that both Shanthi, our cook, and Narayanan, our gardener, spend a good deal of their salaries supporting their extended families, and Dinesh religiously turns over his salary to his mother to spend as she sees fit on maintenance of the entire clan.

At any point in time one or another of our staff needs a loan for some reason, and it is understood in India that good employers should provide reasonable loans to their help at little or no interest. Regular people in India have no other means of borrowing at less than exorbitant rates and no realistic method of saving outside of purchasing gold. Banks are not widely trusted, and, when one has a little extra cash, gold jewelry is bought, which can be sold on a rainy day. Often, however, an Indian might have neither gold savings nor an employer willing to loan money, and so, desperate, turn to a loan shark.

I'm aware that Shanthi owes someone a great deal of money. She casually mentions this fact to me every now and then, perhaps hoping I might volunteer to help her pay off her high-interest loan. Indirectness, I've found, is not a typically Indian trait, and so I wonder why she brings up her troubles in conversation but then doesn't ask me for the dough. She knows—there are no secrets in our household—that I have loaned money to everybody else with the exception of Kutti, who hides from me. Shanthi and I talk about everything. Considering the great and myriad differences separating us, we have quite a friendship, and she has earned my respect. In a fit of goodwill, I ask her to tell me more about her loan troubles.

She owes a loan shark several thousand rupees, an astronomical sum for someone of her means that she can never hope to pay off, considering the terms of the loan: thirty percent interest *monthly*. The interest payment alone is greater than her monthly salary. Shanthi comes to work on time (mostly), does what I ask (except when she knows better), doesn't grumble (she just complains outright), and she more than once keeps us out of big trouble. I want to help her out of her cycle of debt. At the same time, the loan amount is substantial enough that even a good person might be tempted to disappear if she thought she could get away with it. Shanthi doesn't ask me for the money, but I determine I'll talk to Dana about it.

Within days Shanthi comes to me with that look on her face—the one that tells me I should run and hide.

"Saar, I am working for you long time, saar."

"Yes, that's true."

"And I am never stealing from saar. Not one thing. Never!"

"OK. Well, that's good."

"And I am always cooking for saar and madam, saar, and taking good care of babies."

"Just spit it out, Shanthi."

"Spit what, saar? I eat nothing, saar."

"Shanthi, you're a model employee. What do you want?"

The loan shark has come to Shanthi and told her she needs to call in her loan because she needs a dowry for her daughter's wedding. When Shanthi told her she had no money, the desperate lender made her a deal: She'd forgive all unpaid interest and knock ten percent off the loan principal if Shanthi would pay up immediately.

"This is very good opportunity for me, saar."

"So let me see if I understand. You want me to loan you the money. Then you will use the money to pay off the loan shark. And then you will pay me back the money at no interest. Is that right?"

"Saar is very smart, saar."

"Are you patronizing me, Shanthi?"

Shanthi smiles. "I am not understanding meaning, saar."

"Yeah, right. OK, bring the lender to see me."

Within two hours, an impatient woman stands waiting outside. Shanthi was able to get my message to her without leaving the house or calling anyone; again, the servants' grapevine proves more efficient than the telephone. The loan shark wears an ostentatious purple sari of the finest quality. Three gold studs decorate her large nose, and there are more gold bangles on her arms than I have ever seen on one woman. Several gaudy gold chains hang from her thick neck, and bulbous gold rings decorate every chubby finger. She reeks of *nouveau riche* and cheap perfume.

She speaks to me with a haughty air that seems designed to make a point but only serves to betray an underlying insecurity. She has a decidedly slimy air about her—one I don't want in my house— and so, rather than invite her in, I speak to her in the driveway surrounded by Shanthi and her children, who have appeared out of nowhere.

"So you're the one who loans money around here."

"That's right," the woman says with a quick head bobble and a smirk.

"And now you need money."

No smirk. "My daughter is getting married."

"I tell you what I'll do. I'll loan you what you need at thirty percent interest per month."

She frowns. I stare at her in silence. She begins to squirm.

"All right. Let's cut to the chase. Shanthi told me about your generous offer."

"Yes," the lender says, hopeful again.

"It's not good enough."

Shanthi's eyes get wide, and she moves to intervene. "Saar!"

I ignore her and address the loan shark. "Here's the deal. You knock twenty-five percent off the loan balance and forgive all unpaid interest, and I'll give you the money immediately."

The woman recoils in horror. "Impossible!"

"Do you need the money or not?"

No answer. I open the gate, inviting her to leave.

"If you change your mind, come back with the original loan document tomorrow at 10 a.m. I'll have the money ready for you."

She huffs off without another word. Shanthi hasn't looked so mad since her husband, Dom, tried to jump off the roof. Kutti stands next to her, shaking her head in profound disapproval.

"Saar," Shanthi cries, "what are you doing?"

"Shanthi, we take care of each other. Don't I take your advice on everything?"

Shanthi's head bobbles uncertainly.

"This is my area of expertise. You have to trust me on this one."

"OK, saar. I trust you," she says, but she walks off mad.

I talk to Dana about my idea.

"Whatever you think," she says. Dana just floats above these things. "But you should probably get something on paper."

I copy and paste the iTunes terms and conditions into a Word doc and write something at the bottom about Shanthi paying me back. I draw some signature lines and take the document to Shanthi.

"What this, saar?"

"It's a contract saying you will pay me back a little each month at no interest."

"Saar not trust me," she says, feigning great injury.

"Ronald Reagan once used an old Russian saying: Trust, but verify."

Shanthi's expression speaks volumes. "Saar, sometimes I think you very crazy. Really, I am thinking this."

She points to lines for three cosigners. "It is because I am woman you need other people sign also," she says matter-of-factly.

"No. It's not because you're a woman. It's just a business decision."

Shanthi brings the pages back the next morning signed by three male relatives. Of course, this document is entirely unenforceable for a gazillion reasons, not the least of which is that none of Shanthi's folks have any money to give me in case she defaults.

Our friend the money lender arrives at 10:30, the original loan document in hand with Shanthi's "X" on it. I make her write "paid in full" and sign it. I give her the money and tell her that if she ever harasses Shanthi about this loan, I'll speak with my high-level contacts at the Chennai Police Department.

Many Indians, including all the servants, believe that as official Americans, we have all the doors of power open to us and that a simple word to the police will bring all hell down upon them. Of course, we use this erroneous belief to our advantage as necessary.

The loan shark promises we will never hear from her again and departs with a smile.

Shanthi drops to her knees and touches my feet in India's most dramatic gesture of thankfulness and respect, a practice that always makes me extremely uncomfortable.

"Thank you, saar! Thank you!"

I quickly pull her to her feet. "Don't thank me, Shanthi. You're going to pay me back every single rupee. Now let's get back to work."

I wonder if I'll ever see that money again.

CHAPTER 26: FISH YOU WERE HERE

February 7, 2001

OUR FRIENDS ANNABETH AND MAYELA arrive from Texas, and we take everybody to Kerala on India's western coast, one of the highlights of our two years in India. In Kerala we rent a houseboat converted from a traditional rice barge, complete with a crew of three, one of whom is a cook. (Crew's motto: "Beats the hell out of farming.") We cruise the beautiful Kerala backwaters, a network of inland canals running through infinite emerald fields of rice and tiny villages filled with smiling children.

Cole "captains" the boat, and Nina rolls around on a surprisingly clean foam mattress while the rest of us lazily watch the scenery float by. At times the canals are as wide as a lake, while at others we can shake little hands on the shore. We dine on Kerala dishes rich in coconut milk—unlike any Indian food we've ever had in the US— and the flounder-like *pomfret* served with unique light-as-air pancakes called *appams* made from fermented rice flour.

After the spectacular Kerala backwaters, the six of us visit the once-idyllic town of Kovalam. Formerly a tiny fishing village with a long stretch of unspoiled beach, Kovalam exemplifies unregulated development run amok. We arrive to find the Seaview Hotel far out of town and a good half-mile of impenetrable brush from the ocean. We have to go into the town proper to swim in the Indian Ocean and to eat since the hotel's restaurant is out of food until further notice.

Our intention is to stroll Kovalam's main beach, where small restaurants display the day's catch. By the time we get a ride into town it is dark and past Cole and Nina's dinnertime, and they are getting cranky. By the time Dana, Mayela, and Annabeth finally give up searching for the best restaurant and pick one of the dozens of identical places along the shore, I'm getting pretty cranky as well. Not only are the beachfront restaurants identical in style, but they all have the exact same menu, identical down to the color of ink (red) and the character font (Cotillion).

"How about this one?" I moan. "This one looks good."

Dana points at the sign out front. "No way I'm eating at a place called 'Hotel Runs.'" (For some reason Indian restaurants are often called "hotels.")

"I have to agree," Mayela says. "That is a very unfortunate name for a restaurant."

"Well, you have to appreciate their honesty," I add.

We go next door, choose some unlucky fish from the ice, and sit down to wait.

Service is always slow in India by our silly American standards. I think some restaurants are so chintzy they don't buy ingredients until they have a customer at the table. One popular beachfront restaurant in Chennai—popular for its great location, not its food—got so many complaints from foreigners, they finally printed the following disclaimer on their menus: "You must wait at least forty-five minutes for your food from the time of ordering." Since we are aware of this management failure, we always order our food an hour early and go for a swim. They send someone to the beach to get us when it's time to eat.

On this particular night in Kovalam, however, we are hot, tired, and ready to eat an hour before we arrive. I've got jars of food for Nina, but Cole holds his stomach, groaning. Half an hour after placing our order we ask for some bread or chapatti for the children, determined not to be impatient ugly Americans.

"OK, saar," the server says, head bobbling. "No problem. I'll bring it right away."

We get nothing. Nina falls asleep, Cole cries quietly, and Mayela and I are beginning to boil.

I forget the reasons I've learned to like India—the people, the food, the sights, the people—and all the developing-country inefficiencies and irritants that I can normally overlook flood my mind. We ask whether or not our food will be coming soon.

"Five minutes only. I promise, saar, it is coming in only five minutes."

An hour into our wait, Mayela asks to see the manager.

"Manager is not here today," we are told. "Food is coming in five minutes only, madam. I give you my word."

At an hour and fifteen minutes, I tell the waiter we need some food on the table real soon, or we'll take our custom elsewhere. At ninety minutes, Cole falls asleep on an empty stomach.

"Where is our food?" I growl.

"Five minutes only. Five minutes."

I brush past our server on my way to the kitchen. I must find our fish. They aren't on the ice anymore, so they must have gone somewhere! I burst into the kitchen, distressed waiter in tow, and demand our food. Three or four men lounge about the kitchen, apparently without a care in the world. A pair sits at a table playing cards. The kitchen looks like it hasn't been used in months. All eyes are on me.

I'm livid. "Where is our food?"

"Five minutes only, saar! Five minutes."

"I swear, if you say that again I'm gonna—"

"No, just five minutes!"

"Where is our fish? Give it to me. I'll cook it myself."

"Saar, please!"

"If our food is not on our table in five minutes, we're leaving!"

I walk back to our table to general applause. The only other people in the restaurant have given up and left in my absence. I stare at the waiter, counting down the minutes on my watch like a real jerk. With less than a minute left, three waiters jog out of the kitchen with our food.

Mayela, too angry to speak, refuses to be served; only after a good deal of gentle persuasion from Annabeth does she relent. I gently wake Cole. Even though we had each selected our fish and chosen various methods of cooking and accompanying sauces, each fish is exactly the same and smothered with the same super-sweet ketchup-based ooze.

Too ravenous to complain, I take a bite. I feel something strange in my mouth. In fact, my mouth is full of hard foreign objects. I pull one of these things out of my mouth, and then another and a third. My mouth is full of scales!

Not long after our guests depart, I fly to Washington, DC, to take the oral component of the Foreign Service exam a *third* time. While working for Dell, I accrued enough miles on American Airlines to earn a free trip all the way from India to Washington, and this makes the journey a lot easier. *This time* I'm ready. I have taken the test twice before, readied answers for every possible question, and, in addition, the exam itself has been altered to take into account a candidate's interest in foreign affairs, relevant experience, and education. Strangely, the examination had not heretofore considered these three things.

The best thing about the oral assessment is that you get the results the same day; this time I succeed with the minimum passing score. Finally, I will become the diplomat I've always wanted to be, but the hiring process will take many months.

I return to Chennai to find Nina's adoption going nowhere fast. The two other consulate families adopting at the same time have also made no progress. Most frustrating of all is that nobody can tell us exactly what is causing the holdup. We have all submitted reams of paperwork, completed our home studies, and satisfied all the court's requirements. We can't get a straight answer from anyone, so we try to reassure one another and be patient.

ACROSS THOUSANDS OF YEARS, A rigid, hierarchical structure developed in India to order Hindu society. We call this the caste system, and today it divides society into four well-defined *varna* or, literally, "colors." The highest of these is the *Brahmin* varna or priestly varna. Historically, men of this stratum were Hindu priests, and many Brahmin still observe age-old practices in order to maintain ritual purity. The next group is the *Kshatriya* or warrior varna. Traditionally, kings, nobles, court officials, and scribes belonged to this varna. The third layer in the hierarchy is the *Vaishya* varna, to which farmers and merchants belong. Members of the fourth varna, the *Shudra*, performed menial labor.

Each of these varna can be subdivided into many *jati* – a word often translated as "castes." To make a long story short, your presence by birth in one of these castes is the result of actions performed in previous lives, and one should seek to toil and prosper within the constraints of one's caste. In other words, if you were born into a potter's caste, then you should stick to pottery. An oversimplification, perhaps, but this explanation will suffice for finishing my story.

The so-called "untouchables" are alternately known as *harijan*—a term coined by Mohandas K. Ghandi, meaning "children of God" but that many of this group today find patronizing—and *dalit*, meaning "oppressed," which is the term generally preferred by the *dalit* themselves. These folks represent a fifth social stratum below the *Shudra* but technically not part of the caste system at all. They exist outside the caste system and are the poorest of the poor, for whom are reserved the most menial and disgusting jobs. As foreigners we are almost entirely insulated from—and are likely unaware of—the societal rigors and observations of caste. The reader may recall, however, that the woman who cleans our servants' toilets belongs to the *dalit* group.

The Indian government often refers to the *dalit* as members of the "scheduled castes." Included in this category are various tribal and ethnic groups not always fully integrated into mainstream Hindu society, some of which speak their own unique languages. These people are officially known as "tribals" and "backward castes." It is to one of these groups that Nina almost certainly belonged. Caste has come home to roost.

Sometime after Nina comes to live with us, a good Indian friend asks me the question we have been expecting for a while: What caste is Nina? I am surprised no one has yet brought up the issue, because the caste system remains alive and well in India. Many high-caste Hindus have no qualms about espousing their superiority and openly discriminating against Indians of other castes. More progressive Indians like to say caste is not an issue for them, but when it comes to family matters such as marriage and adoption, caste remains an all-important factor. In fact, conventional wisdom has it that adoption is relatively rare in India because the caste of an orphaned child often can't be guaranteed. An Indian friend who has lived many years in the US encourages me to consider my country's long history of racial inequality before casting judgement. Good point.

During our time in India, I've discussed caste many times with Indians of various backgrounds, and I only met one person who said he would not consider caste in his marriage decision. Even he had to admit, however, that the ultimate decision would be made by his extended family, for whom caste compatibility remained a crucial issue. A glance at one of the plethora of matchmaking websites on which Indians search for a mate will easily demonstrate the continued importance of caste; virtually every ad specifies which castes will be considered by the prospective brides and grooms.

Yet, as I say, only one person asks us about Nina's caste. We wonder if this is because Nina is being adopted by a non-Hindu family, or if it is out of a desire not to embarrass us by making us admit our daughter may be of "low" birth. From what I hear, it would be a considerable source of embarrassment to many Indians to admit adopting a child of unknown origin. Indeed, I recall a story in a newspaper of a man who, with the support of his family and local religious leaders, killed his adopted and only child after learning the boy did not come from a certain caste as the orphanage had promised and that the child was likely an "untouchable." This sickened me at the time, and I want to make my position on caste clear to my friend.

"Why do you want to know?" I warily ask. "With all due respect to your religion, I'll tell you right now that to me caste means nothing. I don't believe Nina is any more predestined by God to be a toilet cleaner than I'm predestined to be a basketball superstar. And anyway, no matter what she is or becomes, I'll still love her."

My friend looks around us to see if any of the servants are within earshot. In a whisper, she confides that her mother is a *dalit* who married a very poor low-caste *shudra*.

"I have seen that you adopted this beautiful baby girl and love her no matter where she came from, and so I know I can tell you this," she says. "But you must promise never to tell anyone. Not any of your servants. Not even [a good mutual friend]. Many Indian people say they don't care about caste, but if they find out I am 'untouchable,' it will be very bad for me. I had to lie about my caste when I came to work at [a top-tier software firm]. If I am found out, I will certainly lose my job."

I pick up Nina, who has been pulling on my leg hairs under the table. I plop her on the table and give her a kiss.

"Well," I say to my friend, "your secret is safe with us."

While we grow impatient awaiting news of Nina's adoption, Dinesh's parents begin negotiating the marriage of his older sister, Anjali. The process is amazing in its practicality, and Dinesh keeps me informed of their progress. First, his parents inform friends and relatives Anjali is on the market and that they will be accepting resumes and horoscopes. Next, her parents and uncles conduct an initial screening of suitors, looking at factors such as job stability, family background, caste, reputation, etc. With the remaining candidate profiles, they consult an astrologer who determines the compatibility of each potential match based upon the young people's horoscopes. No candidate is found suitable by the astrologer in the first round, so they start over.

In the second round, the astrologer deems one lucky man compatible with Anjali's stars; it is time for a more intense investigation. Family and friends fan out across Chennai to interview the young man's coworkers, landlord, former teachers, customers, etc., in order determine what type of person he really is. Dinesh explains this is all necessary because once a young lady marries, she practically ceases to be a member of her parents' family and must be content with her lot as a member of her husband's family; to do anything less would bring great shame upon her parents. Too many young women get married, only to find themselves unpaid and poorly treated servants of their husband's extended family. For this reason, he tells me, it is very important to make the right choice of husband the first time.

Soon, the families agree to meet. On the first such visit, the groom's parents come to the home of Anjali's parents. Indian tradition dictates the bride's family pay a substantial dowry to the groom's family upon the marriage of their daughter. Parents often save for a young girl's entire life to amass a sum that will attract for her a desirable husband. This is just one of the reasons that more value has traditionally been placed upon a male child, and it is true that you might hear someone offer condolences upon the birth of a girl. (Dana and I always make it a point to emphasize how blessed we are to have both a boy and a girl.)

Dinesh's progressive family, however, doesn't believe in paying a dowry for their daughter, and they refused to accept one when Dinesh's older brothers got married. They need to ensure this fact is absolutely clear and acceptable to the groom's parents beforehand; in some cases a dowry is agreed upon, but, after the wedding, the groom's family demands a huge sum that the bride's family must pay if they wish to guarantee their daughter's happiness and security within her new family. There are even none too few cases of "kitchen fires" killing new brides where a dowry dispute has been left unresolved.

Next, Anjali's parents and male relatives visit the groom's family home. Apparently, things go well, because an astrologer is soon commissioned to set an auspicious date for the wedding. A date is set, and the couple is officially engaged.

Particularly among the urban elite, it has become quite common for engaged couples to meet in person, under the families' mutually agreed-upon conditions, once a wedding date has been set. In Anjali's case, however, at no time before or during the engagement are the two young lovers allowed to meet, although Anjali's parents indicate a phone call from the groom would be acceptable. Dinesh insists his sister is far too shy to even dream of such a thing.

Dinesh lets on that he is quite impatient to get his sister married off so he can have his turn. He now spends a great deal of his spare time on Indian matchmaking websites, looking at pictures and writing mushy emails to strangers. Anjali's wedding will saddle Dinesh's family with considerable debt that must be paid off before his family will consider his own matrimony. Toward this end, Dinesh turns over all his earnings to his mother, asking only for a small amount to support his online activities. Sadly, due to reasons beyond his control, Dinesh will have to wait more than three years before realizing his dream.

Throughout the search for a groom for Anjali, the *chink, chink* continues at the construction site next door. The bricks-on-the-head women are now ascending to a third level of bamboo scaffolding with the same number of bricks on their heads as before. The building now stands quite tall, and I wonder how much higher they can go without modern scaffolding and machinery.

I often take Nina and Cole in the afternoon to play in the huge pile of sand next to the site. Nina has put on a lot of weight, and it looks as if we will finally get the fat baby we have always wanted. Cole never amounted to much; we are thrilled with Nina's ample rolls of baby fat on her downy-soft thighs. As Nina grows, our household staff insists that she appears less Indian every day. I can only laugh at this.

"No, saar. It true," Shanthi insists. "Why you always laughing me?"

"Because you don't make any sense. You are clearly out of your mind."

"She eat your food. She live with you. She look like you," she says with finality.

"Shanthi, the food she eats will not change the fact that she is and looks Indian."

"NOOO, saar! Saar, listen. I know one Indian young girl. She go to America for ten year. Ten year! She eat only American food for ten year. She come back to India, her mother no recognize her! It true, saar. She is having blond hair and blue eyes and skin like color you. Saar, don't laugh at me. Saar! Saar!"

I clutch my side and try to breathe. "Stop it. You're killing me," I cry.

"Maybe," Shanthi says with a mischievous look and a slight head bobble, "maybe Nina is *your* child, saar."

I gape at her, poised to burst with laughter at whatever issues from her mouth next.

"Maybe," she says, "you have Indian girlfriend, saar."

"Oh, I see. You're suggesting that Nina is the product of an illicit affair I had with an Indian woman, and the whole adoption story is just a ruse."

She thinks about this a moment. "Yes, that's it," she blurts finally.

"Shanthi, did you talk to your other bosses like this?"

"No, saar," she cries in horror. "Of course, I am not doing, saar! Other masters are not so crazy like you, saar. They are firing me, saar, if I do." She flees to the kitchen.

The reader may recall that it was rumored among the servant community that Selvi—our first housekeeper and Shanthi's sister—and I were having an affair. Kind of interesting don't you think? I mean, Selvi quits amid rumors...nine months later an Indian baby arrives...one wonders. For the record, as beautiful as Nina is, she resembles me in no fashion whatsoever.

Speaking of infidelity, one of my weekly playgroup buddies—why don't we call her Susan—runs off with her chauffeur. We learn this when Susan's mother shows up at playgroup one day with Susan's kids and announces that her own daughter has run away to the US with the family driver. Susan lied to a friend of hers at the US Consulate in order to get a visa for her lover, and then they were gone. Not only did she leave her husband high and dry, but she also ditched her kids in the Chennai airport before she boarded the plane.

Her apparently halfwit husband believed her story that she was leaving to care for her sick mother up until the moment the Chennai police called and told him they'd found his boys alone and crying in the airport. Susan had sat the pair—ages four and six—in the departure lounge and told them to wait until she got back from the bathroom. She then boarded a US-bound flight with her new man. When Susan's mother, who was definitely not sick, heard what her daughter had done, she flew to India to take care of the kids until her son-in-law could arrange for hired child care.

Believe me when I say that this gives the tight-knit foreign community in Chennai something to talk about. I imagine that many an expatriate husband never looks at the family driver without suspicion again. For my part, I quickly call a meeting between Dana, Dinesh, and me. Naturally, the servant community learned of this affair almost before it happened, and so it is not at all news to Dinesh.

"Of course, I know everything, saar," he says with a grim head bobble.

I explain to Dana and Dinesh that I know nothing like this will ever happen at our house, because Dinesh would never do anything like that. Dana doesn't find this funny, nor does she find it so when I have my own run-in with temptation. Perhaps it is boredom; perhaps all the talk about fooling around is just too much for some women to handle; perhaps I'm just irresistible. Whatever the reason, I soon find out firsthand how dangerous lonely housewives can be when a good-looking man is around.

CHAPTER 28: AN AFFAIR TO FORGET

A T PLAYGROUP I CONSCIOUSLY AVOID doing anything that could be considered flirtatious. I don't spend too much time with any one member of the group. When we're at the pool, I keep my eyes focused on the children. These women are my friends, and the last thing I want is to be branded an ogling male. I'm very aware that one accidental look down one loose shirt and I'll be in Siberia for good.

A male friend chides, "Man, I wish I could hang out with women at the pool all day."

"Oh, really? I don't even think about it."

"Uh-huh. Sure."

The only one who believes me—my own mother laughed derisively—is my faithful wife, Dana.

But then along comes Helga. (I have changed her name to protect the not-so-innocent.) By all accounts she is a bombshell. I'm not going to lie: She is downright amazing. I guess that's why I was so clueless to all the signals she must have given me before The Incident; I never expected *she* might have the hots for *me*. Of course, many beautiful women, such as my sweet, darling wife, have fallen prey to my charms, but with the bombshell it is all physical. That's how she takes me by complete surprise.

Helga is so perfectly proportioned that even the playgroup ladies stare when she glides out of the pool. Glistening in her bikini, she throws back her waist-length white-blond hair, opens her mouth, and—the spell is broken. It doesn't matter that she speaks perfect English or that what she says is always brilliant—she is, in fact, a rocket scientist—when she speaks in her painfully guttural thick Austrian accent, I can think only of Arnold Schwarzenegger in *The Terminator*. She could say, "Come love me, my hot stud-muffin," and all I would think of is Arnold and wonder when she is going to peel off her face to reveal her futuristic alloy body beneath. Maybe that's what saves me from her, but I like to think it is sheer willpower.

Helga and I see quite a bit of each other at various parties, school gatherings, and assorted functions, but I never see her husband. She has twin boys about two—no one can believe she actually gave birth to them—and we enjoy each other's company at playgroup. As we watch our children play, Helga tells me of her days as a ski instructor back in her home state of Tyrol. We talk of politics and her career having been put on hold because of her husband's ambitions.

It is when we speak of her husband that her face darkens. She complains he constantly travels on business and that when he gets home he never wants to go anywhere. She is unhappy with her marriage and wants someone to listen, and I fulfill that role for her. Dana tells me I get along with women so well because I'm interested in what they have to say. Whatever.

I later tell this story to a female friend, and she asks, "Dana put up with this?"

"We were just talking."

"I would never let my husband hang out with bored housewives all day. Especially rocket-scientist supermodels."

But this is what I do all the time. Even before I got into my latest line of work, I always had many close female friends. In Chennai, without my female friends I certainly would have gone insane with boredom. In any event, I have little opportunity to make male friends. So, ladies, if you're not comfortable with all your husband's best friends being women, don't let him quit his job to take care of the kids. You have to have a lot of faith, and Dana has nothing if not that.

One day, Helga calls during lunch and invites me over. Her invitation takes me by surprise; I'd been to Helga's when she hosted playgroup but never alone. But what am I going to do? Say no? Not on your life!

"Well, I'm just about to put Nina down for a nap. And Cole's over at a friend's. Maybe another day?"

"Actually, I was hoping we could have some adult conversation without kids around. Let Shanthi take care of things. You need a break."

"Of course, saar, I am taking care," Shanthi affirms when I tell her my plans. "I am mother of two children. Very smart."

Something doesn't feel quite right as Dinesh drives me to Helga's. She's lonely and vulnerable. No. I'm being silly. Helga's beauty just has me thinking stupidly; if she were as ugly as sin, I wouldn't think twice of going to her house for lunch. It's my problem; I'm treating her differently simply because she is stunningly attractive. Anyway, I'm a happily married man. What am I worried about? I study Dinesh's face in the rearview mirror for any telltale signs of disapproval: nothing.

When we pull into Helga's driveway, Dinesh parks the car and goes to chat with the house guard. The toys that littered the yard during playgroup are all put up in their proper places. The kids' shoes are arranged tidily at the front door. I notice Helga's car is gone. It's too quiet. I ring the bell, and Helga answers the door herself. Her housekeeper is nowhere in sight. Helga invites me inside and immediately excuses herself and disappears into another room.

"Where are the kids?" I call. No answer. I wait a few minutes on the couch.

"Come here, quick!"

Alarmed, I walk into Helga's bedroom. It smells of roses. She closes the door.

"Where are the kids?"

"I sent them with Shanthi"—her housekeeper's name is Shanthi too—"and Ravi"—her driver—"to the park with Fido. I told them to stay gone for two hours."

My heart is beating so hard, I'm sure Helga can hear it. She takes my hand. My throat is terribly dry, my palms wet. I feel faint.

"Don't be nervous." She puts her arms around my neck and draws close enough to kiss.

"Helga, I don't think—"

She plants one on me. I push her away. My head is spinning, my heart throbbing, and every single person I have ever known from my father-in-law to Miss Bryant, my first-grade teacher—boy, did I have a crush on her—is screaming "*Noooooo!*" OK, maybe there are a few friends from college screaming "*Yeeeeees!*" but they are a very small minority.

"Helga, stop."

She tries again to kiss me.

"Helga, stop. Really."

She backs off, her lipstick smeared. Total silence. I'm afraid to move. (As a senior in high school, I took beginning German for an easy A. I remember literally nothing from that class except for one entirely useless phrase: *Dein lippenstift ist ferwischt.* Of all the things I might have learned in German, somehow these words uttered as a joke by Frau Sather stuck in my mind for fifteen years until, in India, of all places, I finally am presented with an appropriate situation in which to use them, and I blow it because I'm too nervous to think. *Dein lippenstift ist ferwischt* means "your lipstick is smeared.")

Helga takes my hand and leads me to her bed. "I'm sorry. Just sit down here with me a minute."

I don't resist. We sit down beside each other.

"Helga, this is a mistake, I—"

"Make love to me," she breathes in that accent of hers. I see Schwarzenegger, skin peeled off half his face to reveal one beady electronic eye. "My husband is gone. The children are gone. You have nothing to worry about. No strings attached. Your wife will never know."

She puts her arms around me again and pushes me flat on the bed. Her hair hangs over me, putting her face in shadow. I will have a heart attack any second. Her lips pause millimeters from my mouth. "Yes...or...no?"

I'm on the threshold of a decision that could mean fabulous pleasure, a ruined marriage, or both. It is a moment of truth that could change my life forever, but still the decision is easy.

"Let me up. Let me up," I croak, and we are sitting on the bed again. "Helga, I'm going to do you the biggest favor anyone has ever done for you. Good-bye."

She buries her face in her hands. "Could you just hold me for a minute?"

I hold her, and she cries on my shoulder.

"I have to go now."

"You can still stay."

"No, I can't."

"How can I ever face you again?"

"Listen. Don't worry about any of this. As far as I'm concerned, it never happened. Good-bye."

I run outside, nearly ripping the door off its hinges. "Dinesh! Dinesh! Start the car right now!"

Just as I reach the Jeep, Dinesh opens the door, and I dive headlong into the backseat.

"Quick! Drive!"

Dinesh gently puts the car in Drive and heads carefully home as I hyperventilate in the backseat. He never even asks what's the matter—but Dinesh isn't stupid. I, on the other hand, just keep looking for trouble.

❋❋❋

Fresh from the near-fatal run-in with Helga, I go back for more abuse from the Belgian husbands. In addition to the Belgians, there is also a large group of Koreans in Chennai working for a large Hyundai plant. In fact, there are more Koreans at the American International School of Chennai than any other nationality. The Koreans don't come to our playgroup, and we don't see them at the parties most of the other foreigners attend. They stick to themselves and more or less single-handedly support two very good Korean restaurants, one of which has a driving range, and both of which, of course, have karaoke.

The better of the two restaurants has private karaoke rooms that can seat about twenty-five people around low tables on the floor. I come up with the notion of having a playgroup-plus-spouses karaoke party, and the ladies think it's a great idea. However, the prospect of having a party at a Korean restaurant doesn't sit well with many of the Belgians in the group, since they don't want to try any food as exotic as Korean.

"If you want karaoke in Chennai, it will have to be Korean or nothing," I say.

The Belgians reluctantly agree to my plan.

On the night of the party, Dana and I arrive early to ensure all is in order. Unfortunately, six Belgian husbands arrive next, having come straight from work at their office nearby.

"What? You mean we have to sit on the floor?" one asks, and then the complaining begins in earnest.

They critique everything from the tiny ashtrays—of course, they all smoke like chimneys—to the music selection.

"These tunes are from the nineties!"

They sit on the opposite side of the room and talk only among themselves and in Dutch unless they are ready to complain again or insult the waitstaff. Then they switch to English to get their point across. Just when I'm about to ask them to leave, their wives show up and make them behave. In the end, everyone has a fabulous time, but before the party's over, the Belgian husbands have broken four glasses. I suffer flashbacks of my night on the town with the Navy boys. No one can deny the party is a success, though, and my stock among the Belgian men improves as greatly as theirs diminishes with me.

CHAPTER 29: DJIBOUTI CALL

March 2001

WITH ABOUT NINE MONTHS LEFT of our stay in India, it is already time for us to consider our next post. Strange as it may sound, we don't seriously consider leaving the diplomatic corps and moving back home to Texas. There is never a boring day in India, and we are enjoying the diplomatic lifestyle and perks, such as free housing and travel. Dana loves her job, and I'm having a great time taking care of the children; we haven't really formulated a long-range plan for our careers and our children's education.

When the State Department sends us a list of available posts fitting Dana's employment grade, we pore over it with excitement. Instead of having to choose twenty posts from the list as we'd done before being assigned to India, we now have to select only ten. We will then be assigned to any one of those ten locations.

We peruse the list. We could go to Burundi, but we're not really into the genocidal warfare thing. We ask a British diplomat her opinion of Benin, her last post.

"It's lovely. Takes only ten hours to get to Togo to buy silly frills like cooking oil and, say, meat."

Another diplomat recommends we go to Abuja, Nigeria, if we're looking for "the most boring place on the face of the earth."

Papua New Guinea is a good option a friend tells us, "as long as we don't, under any circumstances, leave the house after dark."

"What about Djibouti?" Dana asks a consulate colleague.

"Oh, you'll love it," he says. "Their national bird is the plastic bag." Harsh.

We begin to wonder if we can extend our stay in Chennai, "India's Health Capital," whatever that means. There is a great job as assistant to the ambassador in Moscow, but Dana learns that Moscow suffers 174 days a year of temperatures *below freezing*. She wouldn't live in Moscow even if they made her ambassador.

After much pain, suffering, and gnashing of teeth, we come up with a list of ten posts we can more or less live with. We want to go to Latin America because Dana has never been there, and she wants to learn Spanish. Also, the Latin American countries on our list are more or less in the same time zone as Texas, which will make visits to family less taxing. We place five highly desirable European cities at the top of our list, and five Latin American cities at the bottom. Our logic is that we really have no chance of getting a plum European assignment because everyone else will pick those. Then the department will have to give us one of our next five choices in Latin America, which is where we really want to go.

We're so thrilled at the prospect of a new adventure that it is only toward the end of the bidding process that it hits us: We like India. We'll miss the genuine, gracious people and the delicious food. We've made more new friends in a year in India than we've made since we got married. We've ridden elephants to cliff-top palaces, dined with royalty, and witnessed a wedding on horseback. We've visited the Taj Mahal, remote hill stations, ancient temples, and the spectacular backwaters of Kerala. India's the most exotic place we've ever been. *And*, we found Nina here. It is with both excitement and a heavy heart that Dana turns in our list to her supervisor and we wait to find out where we will go next.

***

One fine day, reliable garbage collection comes to Chennai. Previously, any soul who cared to take the trouble would walk to the nearest major crossroads and dump his or her garbage on the corner pile along with everyone else's refuse. Then, once in a blue moon, two or three barefoot men would shoo away the cows and dogs and shovel a token amount of the garbage pile into a dump truck. These trucks drip a pungent trail as they patrol the city, always overloaded and uncovered.

Yet one day this all changes. A contract is awarded to an international waste management firm to pick up Chennai's garbage and dispose of it properly. Shiny green dumpsters appear on street corners throughout the city, and no one knows what to do with them. The dumpsters are parked on the corners where people have always been dumping their garbage, and for some time the dumpsters sit empty while the populace continues dumping its garbage on the ground. Eventually, a few brave souls begin to use these novelties, and the idea catches on.

Cleaner streets, however, creates a new problem. Dinesh and I witness an angry mob—a not infrequent occurrence—rampaging down a major thoroughfare, overturning all the dumpsters.

"Dinesh," I ask as we flee—Dinesh is my go-to India explainer—"what on earth are those guys doing?"

"Saar, they are turning over the dumpsters so the cows don't starve."

Dinesh has a way of explaining things that makes me feel the answer is quite obvious: With the advent of the dumpsters, the cows can no longer forage on the garbage left on the street.

So, it comes to pass that after the introduction of garbage dumpsters to Chennai, two or three men in bright new uniforms and shoes drive up to the same old garbage corner in their brand-spanking-new garbage truck, complete with a mechanical dumpster-grabbing arm thingy, and shovel the garbage from the ground into the back of the truck just like they had always done. The dumpster stands next to the pile—empty. Garbage in Chennai has come full circle.

Garbage is also responsible for the arrival of the mad Russian from next door. The north wall of our yard is the south wall of a large dilapidated compound. A sign on its door reads "Russian Trade Center," but it is actually a dormitory for the official Russian delegation in Chennai. Back in the day, the Soviets had a large presence in India, which was closer to the USSR than to the West during the Cold War. Since those days the Russian presence in India has diminished dramatically, and their great properties have fallen into disrepair or been leased out. For example, the Russian Culture Center, a few miles away, now houses the American International School of Chennai. On the compound next to us, what once had been a large playground is now a rusted death trap, and a tennis court manages to avoid being entirely overgrown simply because one Russian diplomat personally funds its upkeep. We have little contact with the residents of this compound until the day an angry Russian shows up at our door.

"My name is Sergei," he spits.

Sergei explains that Narayanan, our gardener, has been dumping our garbage on the property of the Russian compound. I go with Sergei and take a look. Sure enough, our garbage has been dumped at the side of the road, but clearly on the Russians' property. It takes a while, but I'm finally able to convince Sergei it won't happen again.

I'd had the luxury until that point of never really giving a lot of thought to our garbage. I knew that Shanthi, as cook and head housekeeper, got first dibs on our throwaways. She went through our rubbish at the end of the day and left the rest for Narayanan. After Shanthi and Narayanan picked it over, the garbage disappeared, and I naïvely assumed Narayanan was disposing of it properly. I was wrong. When I, with Dinesh as interpreter, tell Narayanan he can no longer throw our garbage into the neighbor's yard, he becomes almost as agitated as Sergei. Narayanan asks what he should do with the garbage, and I tell him to use the new dumpsters. He mumbles in toothless accord.

As we leave to take Cole to school the next morning, I notice the previous day's garbage spread on the ground next to the dumpster. Dinesh, driving, sees my expression in the rearview mirror.

"Saar, Narayanan doesn't know what the dumpster is for," he explains.

"In that case," I respond, "kindly explain it to him when we return."

The following morning I'm relieved to find our garbage nowhere in sight. Relieved, that is, until Sergei shows up angrier than before. Under intense questioning, Narayanan admits to having dumped our garbage on the Russians' property as before.

"Narayanan, I like you. You know that. But if you don't stop putting the garbage in that guy's yard he's going to kill me, and then I'm going to be very mad at you."

Narayanan bobbles his head sadly.

"The dumpster is there. Just put the garbage in it. Don't dump it next door. It's very simple."

"Yes, saar."

Two days later Sergei comes back, his face as purple as an eggplant. I'm forced to listen to his tirade for half an hour. I agree with him on all counts. I promise to drink copious amounts of vodka with him at my expense. At last satisfied, he leaves. I won't see Sergei again, but this will not be my last run-in with the Russians. I chase Narayanan around the yard and catch him by the seat of his lungi. Considering he is at least eighty years old, he is pretty spry.

"Tata [Grandpa], get your bags and hit the road. You're fired!"

"But, saar—"

"You can have your job back when you decide to put the garbage where it belongs. Otherwise, have a nice life."

"But, saar—"

"Nope. I don't want to hear it. Good-bye." I shut Narayanan outside the gate, wondering what has gotten into him.

As I had hoped, the next day Narayanan is at the gate.

"I'm ready to put the garbage in the dumpster," he says via Dinesh.

I welcome him back into the fold. "Thank you, Tata. Thank you."

A few days after Narayanan returns, I wake up earlier than usual and look out our upstairs bedroom window. Narayanan, who arrives at work by dawn, is leaving our yard with a full bag of garbage. He walks right past the dumpster, looking about suspiciously. Curious, I throw on my sandals and follow him at a distance. A few blocks from our house, he dumps our garbage at the side of the road in front of someone else's house. He turns and sees me watching him. Neither of us smile.

"Why, Narayanan? Why? Why do you persist in doing this? Why don't you just put the garbage in the dumpster?"

Dinesh is not with us, and so Narayanan understands nothing of what I'm saying. Grumbling loudly in Tamil, he grabs me by the arm and leads me hastily back to the house. Narayanan roughly flips our dumpster on its side. He points inside. He makes wild gestures as if he is sifting through the garbage. He holds his hand about waste high. Exasperated at my lack of comprehension, he repeats this charade several times.

"I'm sorry, Tata. I just don't get it."

Then Narayanan's face opens in a wide grin as he notices something behind me. He spins me around and points at a little boy and girl about five years old sorting through our garbage he has tossed out. We watch them, and soon they run away grinning, their arms full of trash. Narayanan jumps up and down like a schoolboy, pointing and laughing. It dawns on me: Narayanan dumps the garbage on the street so the kids don't have to climb in the dumpster.

At that moment, Dinesh arrives for work and sees us standing in the middle of the street. He walks over.

"Dinesh," I say, "please tell Narayanan to dump our trash on the ground from now on."

"Yes, saar," he says, and I think I see a hint of a smile.

Narayanan takes my hand in both of his and shakes it vigorously, grinning from ear to ear.

So the path our garbage takes to the landfill? After Shanthi and Narayanan get the low-hanging fruit Narayanan sorts it and places it on the street in front of our home, where it quickly disappears. Our neighbors use all sorts of items we have discarded. When I see an elderly lady cooking some liquid over an open fire in one of our Welch's grape juice cans, I am only surprised that something as useful as an empty tin can has gotten past Shanthi. I never look at our trash the same way again.

CHAPTER 30: BANNED TOGETHER

April 2001

S ISTER THERESA FLOORS US WITH news that all foreign adoptions have been indefinitely suspended in the state of Andhra Pradesh. We are speechless. It turns out that Hindu-nationalist politicians are finding it expedient to stoke antiforeigner sentiment in the state. Speeches are made to large groups of angry citizens alleging that babies are being sold to foreigners for body parts or for conversion to Christianity. The local-language press gets on the bandwagon. Finally, the Andhra Pradesh government bows to the pressure and suspends foreign adoptions.

This is our worst nightmare. No one has any idea how long this ban will last and what can be done to overturn it. We are sick with worry. What if this isn't cleared up before we are due to leave? We can't legally leave the country with Nina—she is an Indian citizen with no passport, and we are not yet her legal guardians—but we certainly can't leave her behind! What if Nina is removed from our foster care? What if we aren't allowed to adopt her at all? I'm in weekly contact with Sister Theresa and the orphanage's lawyer, but no one can tell us anything.

The consulate's political section, which routinely translates the local press for its own purposes, passes along to us English-language copies of adoption-related news articles. We nervously follow events and become increasingly alarmed with each passing day. The state government passes a general order prohibiting relinquishment of a child for reasons of poverty, having too many children, or having an unwanted girl child. Silly us, we feel that being unable to care for a child due to poverty and having a child that is not wanted are very valid reasons to seek an adoptive family. Given the high incidence of female infanticide in India, you would think the Indian government would agree.

We read weekly of police raids of orphanages, many of which operate without licenses, throughout the state of Andhra Pradesh. Each raid reportedly turns up dozens of babies that have been purchased or stolen from parents. The same thing had happened two years before, and all foreign adoptions were halted for an entire year. Apparently, that ban did not stop the large-scale merchandising of infants for which Andhra Pradesh is infamous. We see dramatic photographs of parents storming orphanages looking for their missing children. In many cases, biological parents are successfully reunited with their children. So far, nothing specific has been mentioned about Nina's orphanage, and we continue to hold our breath. Meanwhile, Sister Theresa maintains that all is well. We feel sick thinking that Nina might have been stolen from her family or purchased from them. We have to find out the truth.

A multiple-part series runs in India's largest English-language daily, examining the plight of the Lambada people living in rural Andhra Pradesh. A distinct ethnic group, these poorest of the poor have been the target of baby buyers for years. Seeing the desperation of so many around us every day and knowing how much relatively wealthy foreigners are willing to pay to adopt a baby, it isn't difficult to imagine the following, reportedly common, scenario: A family struggling to feed a number of children has yet another girl. Far from being overjoyed, the parents wonder how they will feed another mouth on their wages of less than fifty US cents per day as itinerant laborers. The village "midwife" knows of the family's plight, and so, when the man who buys babies comes to town, she directs him to this family.

The man inspects the girl for any unsightly defects and, finding no visible abnormalities, offers to take the girl off the parents' hands. He makes promises that the girl will be adopted by a rich family and go to school. He offers them a sum of money, somewhere between the equivalent of ten and forty US dollars. The parents thank the man profusely and praise God for their good fortune.

The buyer takes the baby to the big city and offers her for sale to an orphanage with which he has done business before. This agency is run by people who know that rich foreigners will pay literally thousands of dollars in "fees" or "donations" in order to have even a girl child and without regard for the child's caste. Many foreigners will even knowingly adopt handicapped children. The orphanage pays the man two hundred to five hundred dollars for the child.

Meanwhile, an unwitting double-income, no-kids couple in Europe or the United States decides to adopt and contacts an adoption agency, which puts them in touch with an orphanage in India, which has a cute baby girl who needs a home. See what I mean? Not difficult to imagine.

We stare in horror at photos accompanying these stories of people who look just like Nina and are concentrated around the village of Nina's birth. We have to consider the notion that Nina might have to be returned to her biological family. We know we can live with her loss if there are parents somewhere who want their daughter back. We aren't, however, going to give Nina up easily just because of somebody's political game.

After months of anxious wringing of hands, we are told that an investigation will be carried out by the government to determine if Nina's family had, in fact, intended to relinquish her and had done so legally. At the same time, Nina's picture will be published in the newspaper, alongside those of other children undergoing adoption, to see if anyone comes forward to claim her. Only after completion of these two tasks can we proceed to court to finalize the adoption. We are relieved that we may at last be able to put all uncertainty behind us. However, our departure date is fast approaching, and we know things in India don't always move quickly.

One of the other families from the consulate adopting at the same time is enduring a worse nightmare. Both parents work for the US government, and they had been scheduled to leave post several months before us. Yet they couldn't leave on their scheduled departure date because they were caught in the same mess. Finally, the husband left his family behind and went to his new post, while his wife took a leave of absence to remain in India, staying in a friend's guestroom with the baby. Only after months of separation and setbacks did this family finally get a court order granting guardianship, allowing them to leave the country with their child. We are terribly afraid this will happen to us, but at least we don't have to consider the impact on two careers.

Just when we need some distraction, Harish invites us to Simon's beach "resort" again. The Belgians from playgroup and their families are having a cookout on the same day, but we prefer to spend our time with Harish.

"We're supposed to have lunch with a friend," I tell the Belgians.

"Come on," my friend, the hostess, begs. "Just bring your friend with you and stop by for a little while."

Since the party is near Simon's, I agree we'll drop in.

When we walk into the Belgians' party with Harish on the appointed day, you'd have thought we'd thrown a dead crow into the middle of the living room. (I know what I'm talking about. At the age of three, Cole came with us to a party and threw a bloody dead crow on the ground and cried, "Look what I found in the bushes, Daddy!") The men stand in a semicircle around the grill—what I call Universal Barbecue Phenomenon—glaring with furrowed brow as if we've broken ranks by bringing an Indian into their midst. A few of the women greet us and make Harish feel at home, but, for the most part, they receive us coolly as well.

I introduce Harish to the host, and he receives a tepid snub. Ashamed that my so-called friends would behave so rudely, we gather Harish and split, apologizing all the way to Simon's.

"Not to worry," Harish says. "We are like brothers, you and me."

❋❋❋

We give our servants bus fare in addition to their salary, but I know Shanthi and Kutti, who live together, pocket this money and walk the few miles to and from work every day. If the family is ever headed out in roughly the same direction when the pair gets off work, we offer them a ride home. They normally refuse as if we are being utterly ridiculous.

One Saturday, however, we offer them a ride home as we are going out for lunch, and Shanthi happily accepts. (Shanthi and Kutti sometimes work on Saturday mornings, and Shanthi's children, Mani and Priya, usually come to work with them on those days.) Kutti adamantly refuses our offer and runs away down the street as if we have the plague.

Shanthi stares after her. "Kutti very strange, saar. I don't know."

Accepting Shanthi's explanation, we pile into the car—Dinesh has the day off, so I will be driving—and are on our merry way.

Shanthi's grinning children are amazed by the air-conditioned luxury of our American SUV. They "ooh" and "aah" as they gently stroke the upholstery and fiddle with knobs and buttons, rolling the windows up and down. Mani says something mischievous in Tamil to his mother, which his sister immediately and enthusiastically seconds. Mani and Priya are practically wetting themselves with excitement at his idea, but I don't have to know Tamil to see Shanthi doesn't approve.

"What is it, Shanthi?"

"They want saar and madam to come my house, saar."

We are happy to visit Shanthi's home, but I don't want to appear too interested; I fear offending some cultural sensitivity or embarrassing her.

"I see."

"Saar and madam want come my house, saar?"

I'm not sure how to respond, but it doesn't matter; Mani and Priya have already made up their minds. They nag their mother—some things are universal—until she announces she will be honored if we visit. I go back home and grab the only thing handy that can reasonably pass for a gift—a large bag of unshelled peanuts—and get back in the car.

We know Shanthi doesn't live under the best of circumstances. She often complains of living in cramped quarters with many members of her extended family, including her sisters Selvi and Kutti. I'd seen many slums throughout my travels in India, but I'd assumed Shanthi's family does fairly well since she and her sisters have worked off and on as domestics for foreign families for years. I thought I'd seen it all; I was wrong.

As we park on the nearest passable street to their house, Mani and Priya bolt from the car to bring news of our arrival. Shanthi leads us single file past a long line of women down a narrow stinking alley between brick structures with thatch roofs. Cole walks holding my belt loop while I carry Nina, and Dana follows far behind, gingerly stepping around scary objects.

We finally reach the front of the line of women—there are no men in line—and see they are filling jugs at a public water cistern. They eye us in silence. One woman places a full jug on her head and leaves the way we came. We turn a corner and proceed down an even narrower alley between huts of scrap wood and thatch in two inches of mud-slime that reeks of human waste and threatens at any moment to breach the edges of my sandals and mingle with my toes. Visions of our manicured garden and swept patio pass before my eyes. I recall how I had stupidly wondered why Shanthi and her family would want to live in our servants' quarters. Now I get it.

We are now deep in the heart of a small slum village that is all but invisible from the street. The blinking inhabitants of every hovel along our path step into the alley to see us parade past. They gaze in wonder at us, and I can't guess what they must think about this procession of outsiders traipsing into their unseen world. The press of people becomes stifling. I look behind us, only to find the alley hopelessly clogged in our wake. To progress, we have to gently push our way through the ever-growing throng. We are entirely at Shanthi's mercy; the crowd blocks any escape even if we could find our way back to the car.

I shield Cole and Nina as best I can from Indians' annoying habit of forcefully pinching the cheeks of small children; in these close quarters the children are sitting ducks, and they are already crying from the assault.

"Is it OK for us to be here?" I whisper in Shanthi's ear. "I mean, is it safe for us?"

"Saar! All these people my family, saar!"

I see Shanthi's mother at the end of the path, beaming. I know Shanthi's mother because she occasionally comes by our house to speak with Shanthi, always around teatime. (Shanthi frequently receives at our back door groups of women she claims are related to her in some fashion and to whom she graciously offers tea and cookies at our expense.) Shanthi's mother came by once not for tea but to ask me for money to have an enormous tumor removed from her throat. She insisted that I examine the humongous growth before explaining that the free government hospital wouldn't treat her because of her age. Another hospital would treat her, but she had to come up with two thousand rupees. Forty bucks to save Shanthi's mother's life.

All of our servants, except for Dinesh, had needed money for medical expenses at some point, and I typically shared the expenses with them if they could furnish me with a receipt.

"Please giving me two thousand rupees loan, saar, for helping my mother," Shanthi begged.

"No. You already owe me too much money. You can just have the money, but I'm going to write about it in a book someday."

"What you talk about, saar? You no write book, saar. Thank you, saar. You crazy, maybe, I think, saar."

On the day we visit Shanthi's house, her mother stands at the door of her modest hut with several surprised relatives, no tumor in sight, ecstatic at our arrival. She makes as if to touch our feet, but I take her arm instead. People surround us grinning, shouting, feeling our hair, touching our faces. The carnival has come to town, and we are the clowns. Cole and Nina have stopped crying and are now in the arms of strangers. I feel ridiculous for asking if we are safe.

Shanthi ushers us into her hut and presents her uncle.

"He head of family, saar."

We offer our gift of peanuts, and he is overjoyed. The hut is of scrap wood and corrugated tin with a roof of thatch. The dirt floor is raised several inches above the slop in the alleyway, and the ceiling is too low for us to stand upright. A rectangle of bricks in a corner is their stove, and one cooking pot hangs from the ceiling. I notice a few of our discarded household items here and there.

"Where is your bedroom?" Cole asks.

"We are all sleeping together on floor, baby," Shanthi says and gently pinches his cheek.

They have no running water, no toilet, no electricity, no gas range, no refrigerator. They do, however, have a twenty-inch, battery-powered TV they share with all comers. Shanthi explains that every day Mani or Priya takes the spent battery to the battery-recharge man and pays five cents to swap it out for a fresh one. I didn't even know those existed!

We stay and chat awhile before the kids get too hungry and we have to be on our way. Shanthi shouts brusquely at the mob blocking our escape, and the sea of curious onlookers parts slightly. When we get back to the car, led by Mani and a dozen or so boys his age, Dana's white tennis shoes are completely covered with thick putrid ooze, and Cole's cheeks are as brown as Nina's from the tweaking of dirty hands. Mani and his friends insist on cleaning the mud off our shoes with leaves before we get into our car. We thank them all and drive away past the growing line of women queuing for water.

We go to the new Pizza Hut. We never ate there back in the States, but when we learn that mediocre chain has come to Chennai, we feel as if we've won the lottery. We order, and the waiters really put on a show. I mean, they literally put on a show. They stop everything and crank up some bubblegum pop tune and dance in sync in front of our table. You can almost believe they enjoy it from the smiles on their faces, and I can't help but wonder how much you would have to pay the spoiled teenagers who work at Pizza Huts in the US to do those corny dances.

Anyway, I can't pay attention. I'm thinking about the cost of our meal—a week's salary for our servants—and our air-conditioned house and its sanitized tile floors. I think about the big water truck that comes to our wealthy neighborhood and fills our home's private water tank. How can Shanthi walk out of her hovel each day and put up with our silly crises and iron our clothes? Does she resent us? What are we doing?

CHAPTER 31: WHOOPS-A-DAISY

IN AUGUST OF 2001, MY oldest baby begins kindergarten. He is a year too young, but virtually all his preschool friends are heading off to kindergarten, so we let him go. (At the American International School of Chennai they pretty much let parents do whatever they want, including moving kids up or down a grade.) That's how we meet Daisy.

Daisy—sweet, gentle Daisy—who doesn't belong in the dog-eat-dog world of kindergarten classroom management. A single, tie-dyed semi-professional dancer, Daisy had, in her mid-forties, decided she wanted to be a teacher. She attended an ultra-flaky cutting-edge teacher's college in the northeastern US that is remarkable only for its controversial ideas about early-childhood education, and she doesn't believe in "the traditional student-teacher relationship," whatever that means.

Daisy plays herself in caricature; within two weeks of arriving in India, her house is full of stray cats. Within three weeks, it is full of stray cat fleas. She hires a housekeeper but feels guilty about asking her to do any work. When all her jewelry goes missing, I suggest she fire the housekeeper.

"Do you really think Lakshmi would have done it?" Daisy replies, heartbroken.

"Well, she is the only other person who has a key to your house."

"I can't possibly believe a person entrusted with a key to my house would do such a thing."

Two weeks later I call Daisy's house, not knowing she is out of town, and her housekeeper answers the phone. I hear loud music and men's convivial voices in the background.

"Could I speak to Daisy, please?"

Click.

I try two more times and get the same response.

Daisy comes back from vacation, and I tell her what went on in her absence. She listens in horror and hurries home to Lakshmi. I run into Daisy the next day.

"If you're looking for a new housekeeper, I know someone available."

"Oh, no," she says. "Lakshmi says you must have gotten the wrong number."

"I called three times, and it sure sounded like her."

"Oh, well…"

Fine. I have enough to deal with without worrying about Daisy's domestic servant problems. It is Daisy's classroom performance, rather, that concerns me. The American International School of Chennai is a very small school with only one kindergarten class, and the parents all know one another and socialize on a regular basis. In fact, most of the mothers are in playgroup with me. With so many bored housewives and me in town, the school is under close scrutiny, and no one receives more attention than the new teacher, Daisy.

The kindergarten parents figure out quickly there are problems in class, and they are out for blood. I suggest we give Daisy some time; this is her first teaching gig, and she is under intense pressure. Since I appear to be Daisy's only friend—they call me the Daisy-whisperer—the class parents elect me to raise our concerns. I gently suggest to Daisy that she seek some guidance from her department head. She's afraid to ask her boss for help, and so, led by the self-proclaimed Dragon Lady from Singapore, the parents complain to the school.

Daisy sinks into a deep depression. She's afraid for her job. She's lonely and not adapting well to India. Our informal therapy sessions begin to take up a significant amount of my time.

"Tell her to get lost," a playgroup friend suggests.

"Sorry. Not my style."

"Wimp."

Daisy wants children, Daisy wants a husband, Daisy knows everyone hates her teaching, Daisy can't control her classroom, Daisy doesn't like India, Daisy gets sick if she even looks at Indian food—Daisy has menstrual problems! And, OMG, this last one is not something I'm prepared to deal with! Strangely, this is not the first time I've been presented with this type of information, and I have no idea why. Maybe I spend too much time in the company of females. Maybe I'm a good listener. Maybe I give off strange vibes. Whatever the reason, over the years a number of women have felt comfortable discussing their periods' frequency, characteristics, and likelihood of recurrence with me the way my dad likes to tell me about his prostate. I can't explain it; I just want it to stop. I'm not a bad person. Really! OK. I think enough has been said on this subject.

Daisy shanghaies me into taking tennis lessons with her on Saturday mornings, and after every lesson, she insists I help with all sorts of errands.

"It's so hard for me here without a car, you know."

"All right," I say, "but I do need to be going home soon."

"Just one more little stop here. I need you to bargain for me."

"But—"

"Goodness, my breasts are sore. It must be about that time again..."

Hours later, I come home to find Dana and the kids furious with waiting.

"You sure do spend a lot of time with Daisy these days," Dana remarks.

Shanthi, who doesn't bother pretending to not listen to our conversations, makes disapproving clucking noises.

Playgroup friends take to calling Daisy my "girlfriend." I try to fix Daisy up with friends and acquaintances, but each failed romance leaves her unhappier than before.

CHAPTER 32: HOW YA GONNA KEEP 'EM DOWN ON THE FARM?

DANA, DRIVEN BY DINESH, COMES home from work a little early one day and finds Cole, Nina, and me in the front yard playing cowboys and Indians. Cole is the cowboy, and Nina is, well, the Indian, and they are great friends. I am a bad guy of undetermined origin who crawls around on my hands and knees and butts them with my head. Alternately, I am Nina's horse.

"I got some news," Dana says, dead serious.

"Uh-oh. What happened?" I ask, on all fours in the grass. "It's not Sergei, is it?"

Dana grins. "We're going to Paris, baby! I got my assignment today."

I'm dumbfounded. "Paris? I don't understand."

"Paris in France, saar," Dinesh says.

"Yeah, I know where Paris is, smarty pants. I'm just wondering why we're going there."

Dana shrugs. "Don't know what to tell you. It's official."

A second-tour Foreign Service officer was supposed to have no chance of getting a coveted European assignment. We were certain we'd be going somewhere in Spanish-speaking Latin America. And then they assign us to Paris!

"Oh," Dana says. "There's one more thing: We have to move back to Washington for six months while I go to French language training."

This is not in our plans. It means Cole will have to spend the second half of his kindergarten year in Washington. Not ideal. It means we will have to find a place to stay for six months while Dana is in language-training limbo at the Foreign Service Institute. Also not ideal. But who cares? We're going to Paris! With Paris on the horizon, it's hard to focus on our six months still to go in Chennai.

To cope, we compile a list: Top Ten Reasons India Is Better than France. It goes something like this:

10. Indians don't (generally) dislike Americans (as much). (This, of course, is a joke. Indians despise Americans just as much as the French.)
9. Instead of a great big house with a yard, in Paris we'll get a tiny apartment. (This turns out not to be true.)
8. Indians aren't too proud to use English when they know it.
7. Indians rarely smoke.
6. In India we have our own mango tree.
5. In India the police are afraid of us.
4. In France a prescription is required to buy prescription drugs.
3. France enforces traffic regulations.
2. In India, you can have an elephant come to your kid's birthday party for $10.
1. In France we will have to relearn how to wash dishes, drive, lift a finger, etc.

We can think of many more reasons, but I have grown too lazy to write them down.

✻✻✻

Dana, my lovely wife, has moments of desperation where she simply cannot eat any more Indian food. Then bad things happen. In this case, she forces me to eat Mexican food. Mexican food. In India. I strongly advise her against it. I beg to her to reconsider. I hide. This just makes her mad, and so she invites the entire office to go with us to the first-ever Mexican Buffet Night at the Chola Sheraton.

I know that Indians can't possibly understand what Texans expect from their Mexican food, and who can blame them? India's about as far from Mexico as you can get. Yet Dana insists beyond all reason that somewhere on the subcontinent there is a decent enchilada. I feel her pain, but I smell disaster instead of tortillas.

Where to start? Beef. That's a good place to start. There is no beef at Mexican Buffet Night. Understandable — the cow is sacred in India. This is just one reason why *you shouldn't eat Mexican food in India*! Depressed, I order a margarita. I'm not sure what's in it, but there is certainly neither tequila nor lime juice. None of us can figure out what the tortilla chips are made from, but we agree it is something extremely hard.

"What the hell are these?" I ask. I may have cracked a tooth.

"I think they use these as heat shields on the Space Shuttle," someone suggests.

The Space Shuttle chips are served with a bowl of kimchee. I'm about to cry. A banner advertises that two chefs from Mexico have been flown in to prepare the buffet. We ask to meet these guys, if only to ask them how they can insult their homeland in this way.

Two middle-aged Mexican men are produced, and before we can get satisfaction, they don sombreros and serenade us, mariachi-style. What a surreal experience it is for us ten Americans to be in South India listening to "La Cucaracha" and eating lamb and kimchee tacos with avocado chutney. After much debate, we conclude these two Mexicans are enjoying a round-the-world jaunt masquerading as chefs in out-of-the-way Asian cities that don't know any better. In any event, they are swell guys and pretty good singers.

Dana and another young woman are ordered to the state of Kerala to conduct more antifraud investigations, and the kids and I decide to tag along. While Dana and her colleague are logging unheard-of miles in an Ambassador on the all but unpaved roads of rural Kerala, Cole, Nina, and I get a second chance to enjoy the beautiful backwaters of Kerala by boat. The two women spend the week interviewing villagers and amassing evidence of fraudulent statements on green card applications. They roll into each dusty little town and ask the villagers if, in fact, so-and-so are married, exist, etc. All but one of the cases they review turn out to be fraudulent.

When I suggest the consulate should provide security for these little jaunts, I'm laughed at. Cole and Nina can't get into the American Consulate without photo IDs, but it's safe for Dana and a recent college graduate to investigate visa fraud in the Indian boonies? Call me crazy.

CHAPTER 33: SURPRISE, SURPRISE

WE RETURN FROM KERALA TO find Daisy missing me and Chennai ablaze. It seems that Jayaram Jayalalithaa, a convicted criminal, actress, and former mistress of one of the state of Tamil Nadu's most famous politicians, has just been elected chief minister of the state of Tamil Nadu. As soon as Jayalalithaa is sworn into office, she sends the state police to arrest on corruption charges the blind octogenarian former chief minister, Jamal Naidu, whom she has just defeated at the ballot box. Incidentally, Mr. Naidu happens to be the man who orchestrated Jayalalithaa's own conviction on corruption charges only a few years before.

Apparently, when Jayalalithaa's cronies nab ex–Chief Minister Naidu they are a bit rough with him. Fortunately for Mr. Naidu, a TV crew from a local channel owned by Mr. Naidu is present at the arrest and records the whole thing almost as if they knew it was going to happen. Oddly, the other TV channel in town, owned by—you guessed it—Jayalalithaa, fails to report the incident. When Naidu's arrest is aired on Naidu's channel, his followers shut down the city. After a few days of riots, Jayalalithaa lets him go and everything returns to normal in Chennai.

While we were away in Kerala, our hardworking neighbors completed laying the three stories of brick and mortar for the new house next door. This brick is not just a façade; it will be covered with plaster and painted white, and be the walls of the house. The gravel-busting women are nowhere in sight, and the brick-carrying women have gone with them. Now there are only a few people living in and around the workers' huts on the premises. The men spend their long days plastering the walls, while the few women remaining deliver trays of plaster on their heads to them. Still, even after more than eighteen months of living next to us, they stop working to stare at us each time we come home.

For her part, Daisy is having no luck finding a boyfriend, and she wants to talk with me about it. But Daisy won't come around our house; she is terrified of Dana. This works fine for me, because I'm afraid if I ever let her in she might not leave. Daisy invites me to pick her up and go to a coffee shop.

"Madam Daisy is very much liking to talking with you, saar," Dinesh remarks on our way to Daisy's house.

"Yeah, thanks for the observation, Sherlock."

"But saar is not like to talk to Daisy?"

"I didn't say that. Just be happy you get to wait in the car."

"What an insensitive brute," you say? Be kind; I'm just venting. I spend countless hours counseling Daisy and sympathizing when her biorhythms move out of sync or Aunt Flo visits.

"I don't know, Greg," she says as we sit in a coffee shop a stone's throw from the pungent Adyar. "I feel like I've lost touch with my ancient soul. I guess it's just that time of the month."

Ugh.

***

As we drive ourselves nuts worrying about the lack of progress on Nina's adoption, we are well aware that time is running out for us in India. We spend our free time shopping for mementos and planning trips to see the many interesting sights we have so far missed. At work, Dana is involved in a nearly complete renovation of the consulate facility. We won't be in India to see its completion, but Dana has been tasked with purchasing all the furniture for the new consular section. Dana, as parsimonious as ever, resolves to save the taxpayer some money by sourcing the furniture in India, even though that makes the job more difficult for her. After several weeks of ripping the arms off shoddy desk chairs and listening to the promises of furniture salesmen, Dana makes her final decisions only after personally testing all the chairs, desks, and filing cabinets.

This thoroughness returns to haunt her more than three years later. After we leave Paris and move on to our third post, Phnom Penh, Cambodia, a workplace health and safety inspector comes to the US embassy in Phnom Penh for a short visit. This gentleman lectures the embassy staff on the importance of proper desk height and chair comfort in avoiding all sorts of work-related ailments such as chronic back pain. He cites an interesting example of how not to purchase office furniture. He tells a tale of a six-foot-tall first-tour Foreign Service officer in Chennai, India, who purchased an entire building full of chairs and desks for a staff of mostly Indian women who were at least a head shorter than she was. This expert describes how these ladies are forced to sit on the edges of their seats without leaning back all day, their feet barely touching the floor. Dana privately identifies herself to him as the very woman mentioned in his story, and the expert explains she is infamous. Every talk he has given for the past three years has included the details of her notorious purchase.

When Dana is not out looking for inappropriate furniture during our last summer in Chennai, she's at home in bed with various ailments. It seems as if she never goes to work, and that interferes with my social schedule. First she catches a cold or something and never seems to get over it. Then she gets something else. She is always weak and tired, and then one morning Dinesh and I—not sure what Dinesh is doing there— find her on her knees in the bathroom with her head over the toilet bowl.

"Dana, I can't believe it."

[retching] "Believe what?" [retching]

"You're pregnant, aren't you? I can't believe it. After all this, you're pregnant."

[retching again] "That's impossible. The doctor says it's impossible." [retch]

"The doctor's an idiot. That's why you're feeling like this. That's why you've got morning sickness."

"No! I'm not pregnant...well, you know, I guess I could be."

"You'd better get tested."

Dana pulls her face out of the toilet bowl and leans against the wall. "Open the medicine cabinet. There's an old home pregnancy test in there."

I give her the test and help her up off the floor. Dinesh looks concerned.

"Here," I say. "Pee on the stick right now."

"Could you *please* take Dinesh and get the hell out of the bathroom?"

Exactly one minute later, Dinesh and I find out I will be a father of three. My wife, reportedly infertile, unable to conceive, and otherwise reproductively challenged since the birth of our first son, is now with child. After two years of infertility treatments and a doctor telling us Dana can't conceive again without surgery, my wife is preggo. Typical.

"Does this mean we can get a minivan?" I ask. "I want a minivan."

"Shut up," Dana cries, throwing the testing stick at me.

I dodge. "Gross!"

"And I thought you hated minivans!"

Cole is thrilled to hear the news, Nina is nonplussed, and Dana and I are numb (but it's a happy numbness). Interestingly, another consulate family, in the process of adopting after many years of infertility treatments, is expecting a baby as well. Daisy congratulates us before sinking into an even deeper depression. I refuse to accept responsibility for Dana's condition and immediately go in search of a scapegoat.

Shanthi beams with triumph. "We know you and madam are trying to make baby, saar."

Geez, that's a comforting thought. "Really?"

"And so we go to temple and praying for it."

"I see. And so, *voila*! Dana's pregnant?"

"Yes, saar. I'm thinking it is like that, saar."

Dinesh bobbles his head in agreement. "Yes, saar. We go to temple and pray for your making baby. Saar is not remembering?"

This sounds vaguely familiar; a year or so ago they had mentioned something about it. "Well, that's sweet of them," I thought at the time, their praying for our fertility. But after Nina arrived, I guess I forgot to ask them to go back and call the whole thing off.

"Saar," Shanthi says, "I am needing day off to go to temple and walk on fire."

"I'm sorry? Did you say *walk on fire*?"

"Yes, saar. Walk on fire for God."

Walk on fire for God. I'd like to see a bunch of good Southern Baptists do that. Honestly, how many of you even know someone who has walked on fire? And, as if that isn't enough, Shanthi plans to stick metal rods through her tongue for good measure. But wait! There's more: Dana and I are indirectly responsible for Shanthi's need to self-mutilate. Apparently, Shanthi promised God that if Dana got pregnant, she would walk on fire and stick metal rods through her tongue. Now it's time to pay up. Whoa! Pretty heavy stuff. I'm kind of afraid *not* to give her the day off.

"Wow, Shanthi. That is the best excuse for a day off ever."

Shanthi is expressionless. "It is only normal, saar."

I look at Dinesh. "Yes, saar, normal," he says.

"All right. Sounds legit."

"And," Shanthi adds, "Kutti is needing day off too, saar. Kutti can only working when I am working."

I have given up asking. "Sure. Take the day off. And Kutti too."

But now for the truly bizarre: Dana is trying to kill me! Even before she read this book and after all I have done for her. Since everything from surgery to shoeshines is dirt cheap in India, many expatriates do things they can't afford back home, such as skydiving, golf lessons, and plastic surgery. A number of foreigners we know have gotten vision-correcting surgery at a small fraction of the US cost. Dana suggests I get my eyes fixed too, but I just can't let someone cut on my eyes in a country that lets cows snarl traffic for hours. Then—you are not going to believe this—Dana rather timidly suggests—you are really not going to believe this—Dana suggests I save us some money by *getting a vasectomy in India*!

"Dana, have you seen what they did to the dumpsters? No. No way. Not getting a snip done here."

Look, I'm not saying India doesn't have great doctors. For those who can afford it, India has excellent medical care. (Just like in the US.) Sadly, this leaves several hundred million people to rely on cheaper but rationed care in poor hospitals. The cost of care is not the issue for me. I'm not into the medical tourism thing, because, if I'm going to let someone near the family jewels, I want to be able to sue the hell out of them—American style—if anything goes wrong.

For other less critical medical needs, we rely on Indian medical care that is so cheap we don't bother to file any insurance claims.

Ultrasounds cost only three dollars, so whenever we feel like taking a look at #3, we pop down to the neighborhood clinic and have a peek. Because of the terrible female infanticide problem in India, it is illegal for a doctor to divulge the sex of a baby before it is born.

"Congratulations, you're going to have a boy," the doctor says on our first visit.

I give her a dirty look. "Uh, I think you weren't supposed to tell us that…and, anyway, I guess we wanted to know…"

"Yes, yes," the doctor says dismissively, "but there is something we need to discuss."

Apparently, an enlarged fold of skin on our baby's neck indicates an increased chance of him having Down syndrome. We go home in shock and talk of nothing else while Cole and Nina take their customary naps. Can we cope with the challenges of raising a child with Down syndrome? We will have to wait several more weeks before another ultrasound can tell us more.

CHAPTER 34: THE RUSSIANS ARE COMING! THE RUSSIANS ARE COMING!

ONE NIGHT ABOUT MIDNIGHT A large explosion shakes the house: *Boom!* I sit up in bed, thinking I must have been dreaming. *Boom!* Nope. Not dreaming. Apparently, someone is shelling The Flame. Dana's snoring lightly. I grab the emergency radio, a hotline to the consulate, to call for help. The radio is dead.

"Damn, we've got to charge this thing," I cry.

Dana rolls over, putting her back to me. "Shut up!"

She isn't always the nicest person when her sleep is interrupted. Seriously. Don't wake her up.

"Shut up? Someone is bombing us!"

Dana pulls her pillow over her head.

Boom!

I throw some clothes on, grab Uncle Laried's WWI bayonet from the closet, and race out the back door, determined to kick some butt.

A rocket whistles overhead and explodes nearby. *Boom!* I hit the ground. My ears are ringing. The rockets are coming from the Russian compound next door. Holy crap! After all these years the Russians have finally declared war, and it starts in my backyard.

Between incoming missiles, I hear laughter coming from the top of the Russians' dilapidated dormitory. I march out our front gate, bayonet in hand, and head to the Russians' front door. I bang on their compound's gate with my weapon. An ancient Indian security guard opens the gate, snaps his heels, and salutes.

"Uh…at ease…uh…comrade. But what the hell is going on?"

He salutes and waves me in. I enter the Russians' diplomatic compound, wondering if I should've left the bayonet at home. The guard returns to his box by the door, apparently unconcerned by my presence. I approach the nearest building and try the door: locked. A second building is open, but it's completely dark, and the light switch doesn't work. It's like a completely deserted hotel. No way I'm going in.

"Hello! Hello! Anybody home? Cease fire!"

My behavior has caught the attention of the revelers on the roof. They are laughing and pouring beer down on me.

"Hey! Could you cut it out with the bombs," I yell up at them.

They disappear. A minute later, six or seven large men in Russian sailors' uniforms spill drunkenly out of the building. They are followed by an equal number of tall blond women in evening gowns and high heels, drunk as well.

"Are y'all crazy? What are you firing at my house? It's after midnight," I shout at them. What is it with me and sailors?

They look at one another in stunned silence and then, as a group, burst into raucous laughter. One of the men admires my bayonet. Pulling the women along behind them, the sailors stumble out the gate of the compound, laughing all the way. The last one gives me a very hard pat on the shoulder and a half-empty bottle of vodka. They disappear in a convoy of auto-rickshaws, leaving me waving good-bye. The old man snaps to attention, and I hand him the vodka. He seems impressed. I go home to a snoring Dana.

The morning after the Russian attack, we return to the doctor's for another ultrasound, and there continue to be signs that our child may have Down syndrome. The doctor recommends another ultrasound in a few weeks' time. If that proves inconclusive, he says, we should consider amniocentesis, a relatively risky procedure that will tell us definitively if the baby has Down syndrome. By this time, I have come to terms with the fact that our baby and we might have to live with this condition. I begin to have confidence that we not only can handle it but also that it will not ruin our lives.

✳✳✳

A few weeks later, when I'm still dealing with PTSD from the trauma of the Russian nighttime rocket attack—the Russians' official response is "fireworks gone awry"—my sleep is interrupted again. I'm dreaming of a juicy well-marbled rib-eye steak, when something hits me on the head. I open my eyes. Dana reaches over and hits me.

"What did you do that for?"

No response.

"Well?"

The doorbell rings, and Dana swats me again. Then it rings again. And again. Someone is pounding on our front door. I squint at the clock: 5:30. I roll out of bed, put on some shorts, and stumble downstairs to kill this person. I look out the peephole. No one. Great! Someone is playing a joke. A loud knock startles me. I throw open the door.

"Now, listen you—"

Narayanan, our octogenarian four-foot-tall gardener, runs under my arm into our living room wielding a machete and a broom. He commences screaming and flapping about, waving his machete wildly in the air.

"Dana! Honey! Tata's finally gone off the deep end," I yell. "What do we do?"

I figure I should try to calm him down, but I don't like the looks of his machete. Narayanan drops to the floor and peers under our furniture.

He pokes his broom under the couch and our entertainment center. He stomps his bare feet and kicks things. He sprints into the guest bathroom. There are shouts and the unmistakable ear-shattering sound of Narayanan's machete striking our bathroom tile again and again. Silence.

I peek into the bathroom. Narayanan is bent over behind our toilet. "Tata? Are you okay?"

Narayan turns and shoves the head of a large cobra in my face. "Ha!"

I shriek and stumble backward in horror.

Narayanan explains to me with melodramatic gestures that he had been working outside early that morning, when his activities disturbed the cobra that then slithered across the yard and under a side door of the house. He found it coiled up behind the toilet waiting for the morning's first customer. I decide to let Tata off the hook for waking us up.

All of these trials conspire to make me feel older, and when Cole— not quite five—has his first telephone conversation with a girl, I know my baby is growing up too. He asks one night if he can call Camilla, a school friend, and so I help him dial the number. Beside myself with curiosity, I stay where I am.

And then he breaks my heart. "Dad, I'm trying to have a private conversation. Can you go, please?"

Like any reasonable parent, I sneak into my bedroom and quietly pick up another receiver.

"May I speak to Camilla, please? I am Cole. Greg is my father."

I smile. He's using his manners. And I'm his father.

"Why not?" answers Camilla's mother.

"Hello, Cole," Camilla says. "Why are you calling me?"

"Well…you see…I want to talk to you about…about that marriage thing…you see."

"What?"

"Don't you remember? We're supposed to get married…you know…we talked about it…"

"Oh yeah," she says. "That was yesterday."

"You still want to…right? Get married, I mean."

"I have to go to bed."

"Oh."

"I'm hanging up now. Good-bye."

"Well…good-bye. We can get married soon, I hope."

Click.

✵✵✵

Nina has now been with us for almost a year; Cole can barely remember what it was like before she joined us. At a little over eighteen months old, officially, Nina still shows little interest in walking. She crawls around the house—still backward—at a remarkable speed and gets into things Cole would never have touched. She eats unbelievable amounts of food. Her stomach becomes so enlarged after meals, I'm afraid she might pop. Cole is trying to teach her to say, "I just wanna be your teddy bear."

On our way to playgroup one morning, Cole, Nina, and I get on an apartment elevator with some of our playgroup buddies.

"Quick! Close the door before any Indians get on," one of the Belgian housewives, Boukje, says, to the amusement of her friends.

I can't believe my ears. The door closes.

"Wait. Open the door. We need to get off," I say.

"What's wrong?" my oblivious friend asks.

"You don't want Indians on the elevator, so we're getting off."

Boukje looks as if she's messed her pants. "Oh, I didn't mean Nina," she says reassuringly, as if that solves everything.

"Well, she's Indian. So what exactly did you mean?"

The door opens, and we all get off the elevator in front of our hostess's apartment. The question is never answered.

At playgroup Nina competes for the title of Model Baby, but at home she cries. A lot. Actually, she wails, and her wails bring the house to a standstill. They peel paint off walls. Sometimes she cries most of the day. Has she been scarred by some terrible experience in her past? Am I doing something wrong? Cole rarely cried and went everywhere with us since the day he was born. We rarely take Nina out to eat with us or to parties, because she goes ballistic at the drop of a hat. The doctor has no suggestions.

I learn there are few economies of scale when it comes to raising children. Two children mean twice the work.

"Why don't you just hire a nanny?" a friend asks.

"No way. I just quit a good job to take care of the kids." But those wails!

As much as I hate to admit it, pride is also a factor in my decision not to hire more help. Here I am, a lone father trying to survive in a world of mothers, dealing with ridicule, suspicion, and assumptions of incompetence. To hire someone—a woman, no less—to take care of this baby for me would be a surrender too humiliating to accept. I have to prove to myself and the world that I'm not only über-competent but also comfortable in my nontraditional role. I have to be Super Dad. My children must be twice as well-behaved, I have to look twice as happy, my house has to be twice as clean, and my snacks must be twice as healthy when it's my turn to host playgroup. I have to be more calm, cool, and collected than my female compatriots or else I prove the naysayers right. I can speak only to Dana of my feelings of boredom, stress, and fatigue, and all this posturing is wearing me out.

September 11, 2001

W E COME HOME LATE FROM a dinner party and turn on the TV to see the second plane smash into the World Trade Center complex in New York. Instead of thinking, "How could someone do this?" I am amazed no one had done it sooner. I guess that makes me a pessimist. As we stand with our mouths open, watching it all live on CNN, the phone begins to ring. Consulate friends call to see if we have heard the news, relatives call from the US to see if we are all right, the regional security officer calls to tell us the consulate will be closed the next day, and Indian friends call to express their sympathies.

For a week, the consulate is inundated with condolence calls and gifts of flowers. Dinesh asks me to explain how someone can hate our country so much; Shanthi personally vows to get revenge on our behalf. Kutti nods in silent agreement. The Prince of Arcot offers his palace as the site for a memorial service. The consulate remains closed for several days, and the talk turns to questions of evacuation of consulate dependent family members if the United States goes to war in Afghanistan.

Beginning September 12, our home has twenty-four-hour police protection. On September 15, the police start asking for money—on top of the morning and afternoon tea we already give them—a request we kindly refuse. When not sleeping, the two or three plump officers armed with vintage rifles laze in lawn chairs we provide them, chewing betel nut and playing cards. But they are almost always sleeping. Once, arriving home in the middle of the day, we stop our car at the gate, unlock and open the gate, pull into the driveway and get out of the car, and close and lock the gate without waking even one of them.

As representatives of US interests abroad, we are, after 9/11, on high alert. When I ask myself, "If I were a terrorist and really wanted to hurt someone, where would I attack?" I don't have to think hard. For some months, I have been complaining that security at the American International School of Chennai is dangerously lax. Any person can walk onto the premises without challenge, and the events of 9/11 underscore the need to beef up security. Identification cards are issued to all parents, and to mock these half-efforts, I make it a point to get on campus every day without wearing mine. No one ever notices. When we leave India, virtually nothing serious or effective has been done to protect this softest of targets.

We go for a third ultrasound.

"Your baby's measurements are virtually normal now," the doctor tells us. "Based upon this, your baby almost certainly does not have Down syndrome."

Strangely, instead of feeling relieved, I take the doctor's words unemotionally, as a simple matter of fact. Dana and I are quiet as Dinesh drives us home, and we don't talk about it after that.

Dinesh's sister finally gets married, and it isn't long before Dinesh's parents begin planning his nuptials. Dinesh explains to me that an Indian considers the appropriate and auspicious marriage of his or her children one of life's major goals. Only once all the children are successfully married can one embark on the last of life's great missions, that of removing oneself from the ways of the world as preparation for death.

Dinesh confesses to me that all his time spent searching for a bride on the internet has been fruitless because he has not been honest when registering himself on matchmaking websites. Dinesh lied about his profession because most Indians who have the wherewithal to have internet access are beyond his economic and educational class. He feels no one will be interested in a personal driver, so he has called himself a "computer professional." In order to improve his prospects for a good marriage, Dinesh considers all sorts of schemes for achieving financial success and runs them by me.

"Dinesh, your mother and father will find the right woman for you. Any woman would be lucky to have you."

"Thank you, saar, but, no, saar. I must improve my station," he says.

Although I think Dinesh is selling himself short, I jump for joy when an opportunity arrives to help him achieve a greater level of job and income security, which he believes will improve his chances of landing a plum bride. I hear from a friend that the British Deputy High Commission—the Brits' version of a consulate—is looking for a full-time driver.

This is the kind of job every personal driver like Dinesh dreams of. It comes with job security, benefits, and a salary about double what a family can pay. We will be leaving India in three months, and ensuring our servants find work upon our departure is of great concern to us. I simply call the Brits and tell them they'd be crazy not to hire Dinesh. This lands him an interview, and, of course, he gets the job.

We knew it had to happen sooner or later. Dinesh, who guided my parents and niece around South India, who helped me get a suicidal maniac off the roof, who recovered our stolen auto parts, who waited patiently in the heat for hours while our guests power-shopped, who changed diapers and lightbulbs, washed dishes and took Cole to pee on the side of the road, has to go. For the record, Dinesh can't sew, and he once showed up for work five minutes late.

Dinesh hangs his head and gives me the news. "But I am not taking the job, saar."

"Dinesh, not another word, please. You have to consider your future."

He starts to cry. "No, saar."

"We are leaving India in three months, and you will be unemployed. It might be months before you find work again."

"No, saar. I will work for saar and madam until they are leaving India."

"Who's going to marry you, Dinesh, if you don't have a job? If you have a job at the British Deputy High Commission, girls will be lining up to marry you."

This hits home. After more emotional discussion, Dinesh relents. During his last week, he mopes about his work. On his last day, he is an emotional basket case. When I have to ask him to turn over the car keys, he breaks down and cries on my shoulder. Me? I'm cool and aloof. From that day until we leave in December, Dinesh comes almost daily for a visit. One night at ten o'clock, I find him washing our car.

"What you are you doing, you crazy Indian person?"

"Car is dirty, saar."

"You can't call me 'sir' anymore. You don't work for me now. We are just friends."

"Yes, saar."

Dinesh becomes our new nighttime babysitter, and it isn't clear who enjoys that the most. Clearly, he is having trouble letting go. We don't really mind.

With Dinesh out of the picture, Dana begins carpooling from work each day with a colleague, Donald. As Dana arrives home from work one afternoon, Donald's driver points out that the same white van has been following them home from work each day for a week. The van is parked thirty yards down the street facing The Flame.

I peek out the gate at the van. "Who do you think they are?"

"Maybe IB, saar," Donald's driver, Vijay, says, referring to India's Intelligence Bureau.

"Where are you going?" Dana asks as I run toward the house.

"To get a camera," I yell over my shoulder.

When I return with an old 35mm film camera, she's got that look on her face that wives get when their husbands are about to do something really stupid.

"Come watch," I say. "This is going to be good."

I put the camera in my pocket and walk casually out the gate as if I'm going to buy a mango or throw my household garbage on the corner pile. I stay on the opposite side of the street from the van and gaze past it, pretending not to be watching. When I get directly opposite the van, I whip out my camera.

The van's occupants have apparently been watching me closely, for the very second I turn toward them, their engine starts. I bound across the street, snapping pictures on the run—or I would have if the camera had actually had any film in it—and have just enough time to thrust my head in the open window of the van, stick out my tongue, wag my head, and scream like a madman before they peel out. At this point, I have to let go or ride along hanging on the outside of the van. I choose the former.

The van speeds down the road, dodging pedestrians, toward a large mound of gravel inexplicably piled in the center of the street. They shoot over the pile and land in a spray of sparks before screeching around a corner. Dana and Donald wave to them from our front door. I throw a Hail Mary with a chunk of brick and just manage to nick their bumper before they disappear. We never see them again.

Full of adrenaline, I race inside and call John, the consulate's regional security officer, and tell him what happened. Shockingly, not only does he not praise my heroic efforts at running off a would-be Osama bin Laden but he even has the gall to suggest that it was a foolish and dangerous thing to do and that I should refrain from such behavior in the future. He obviously doesn't understand that we housepersons need a little adventure once in a while.

"I guess it could've been a little dangerous," I acknowledge.

"Well, duh," he says.

"Man, you're such a Debbie Downer."

CHAPTER 36: ALL POLITICS IS HELL

ARTICLES CONTINUE TO BE PRINTED in the local press detailing the sordid nature of the adoption business in the state of Andhra Pradesh. Daily accounts of girl babies being sold by parents to agents who in turn sell them to orphanages who then sell them to foreigners sicken us. Nina's orphanage is often mentioned by name in the press, and we are in frequent contact with Sister Theresa, who assures us that all her dealings are aboveboard. Sister Theresa maintains that her orphanage is being targeted because it is a Catholic charity and that investigators scrutinize her records more closely than orphanages run by Hindus.

"Let them come," she says. "God will protect us."

Eventually, nearly every private orphanage in the state closes, while Sister Theresa's remains open despite the scrutiny.

Given the state of politics in Andhra Pradesh, it is entirely likely there is a bias against non-Hindus when it comes to investigations into the adoption racket. Indeed, the very fact that non-Hindus are allowed to adopt Indian children at all is a political hot potato. Furthermore, it is incorrect even to use the term "adopt" in this instance because, according to Indian law, Muslims, Christians, Buddhists, and Zoroastrians are not allowed to adopt a child outright in India but can only be granted legal guardianship. Hindus are allowed full adoption rights. Also, according to Indian law, foreigners can only apply for legal guardianship of a child after it has been certified that no Indian Hindu family wants the child, and then preference is to be given to other Indians and people of Indian origin residing abroad.

A local-language daily begins publishing, in a series of articles, confidential records that prospective adopting families have filed with the Andhra Pradesh state ministry in charge of adoptions. For example, one article, stating the full names of the people in question, claims that many of the couples from abroad wanting Indian babies are "too old" to have small children; some couples, it says, list "minister" or "missionary" as an occupation—supposed evidence of a plot by zealous Christians to convert Hindus to Christianity through adoption.

To underscore the supposed unsuitability of some prospective parents, their medical histories are disclosed or they are identified as physically handicapped in some way. In the last paragraph of the last article in the series, I see something that leaves me dumbstruck: "Even Dana Williams, Vice-Consul at the American Embassy in Chennai, got her hands on one of these children."

Obviously, we are very concerned. What if some Indian politician decides to remove Nina from our care simply to show he can stand up to "important" foreigners? What if we are used an example? What if an angry mob shows up at our door? I feel as if we will never be safe until we leave the country. But we can't leave; not without Nina. I fantasize aloud about sneaking across the border into Pakistan—more than a thousand miles away—and buying Nina a stolen US passport on the black market so we can hop on a plane.

"That would be called kidnapping and would break about a hundred other laws," Dana counsels, distraught but still sane.

"But it's *not fair!*"

"We'll just have to wait it out."

Finally, with only two months left to go in India, we are informed the investigation into Nina's relinquishment has been completed. The investigator determines that Nina's biological parents did, in fact, wish to relinquish her and did so legally. This is the best news we have heard all year, and we celebrate that night. We had never wanted to break the law or adopt a child whose parents had not intended to relinquish her. At last, our case will go to court, and, hopefully, we will be able to leave the country on time.

Buoyed by this good news, we go to our second International Women's Association charity Christmas party. Our friend Daisy, the kindergarten teacher, goes with us, and I even manage to fix her up with a State Department contractor who is in town for a week working on some computer stuff. As soon as I introduce them and see the man's predatory gaze, I know I've made a mistake. Like a lion preys on the weak, this man immediately senses Daisy's vulnerable nature and exploits it to get what he wants. They make fools of themselves, cavorting drunkenly on the dance floor, kissing passionately, hanging all over each other—in front of virtually the entire expatriate community of Chennai and many of the parents of Daisy's students.

"Good for Daisy. She could use this," a friend says, but I can't help but feel it's going to hurt.

Daisy's new beau excuses himself to "piss like a racehorse," and I pull her aside.

"Are you sure you know what you're doing?" I ask while Daisy tries to focus on my face.

"Greg Buford! You're jealous," she squeals and stumbles off to find her man.

Daisy calls me the next day to tell me of the rest of her night in too much detail. She is happier than I have ever seen her, she is in love, she is Daisy. Her euphoria turns to heartache one day later when the contractor unceremoniously dumps her.

Daisy is inconsolable. "I feel so betrayed. I just can't believe it."

"Daisy," I say, as gently as possible, "you only knew him for two days. Are you sure you should feel betrayed?"

"He told me he loved me." And then she starts to cry.

❋❋❋

Dana is now showing quite nicely, and Nina remains in official limbo. Even though all requirements have been met, we still don't have a court date. In this final step, the judge will review all the documents and sign a certificate legally making us Nina's guardians. We can't apply for Nina's passport and leave the country without this certificate. The stress of preparing to leave, under the best of circumstances, is enough to make us crazy, without the added pain of having to make contingency plans for me and the kids to stay behind in India if everything isn't finalized in time.

These days are a frantic blur of calls to our lawyer, Sister Theresa, and the American Consulate. The consulate is assisting many Americans in the same boat, most of whom are living in the US and don't even have foster care of their babies. We are the lucky ones; at least Nina is with us. To make things worse, in their terribly frustrating and characteristically Indian desire to please despite the facts, Sister Theresa and our lawyer daily make promises about when we can expect to reach the next milestone in the guardianship proceedings. I'm *really* about to lose it. On at least one occasion, in my certainly frustrating and characteristically American habit of throwing what my grandmother would call a hissy fit, I all but shout at our lawyer to stop telling us what she thinks we want to hear.

"Last Thursday you said the court clerk told you we would get a court date by Monday. Today is Tuesday. The week before you said you were one hundred percent sure we would get a court date by last Wednesday. Today you are telling me we will certainly get a court date by Friday. Just stop it! If you don't know, just tell me you don't know. If you don't have any idea when we will go to court, then tell me you have no idea! *Just tell me the truth!*"

I slam down the phone and call Dana at work to tell her I'm going to fire our lawyer and that I'm "sick and tired of you throwing your damn bras on the bedroom floor and leaving little blobs of toothpaste in the bathroom sink," at which point *she* hangs up on *me*. An hour later, I call them both back and apologize, and our lawyer tells me she has been informed by the court clerk that we will absolutely positively have a court date by next Thursday.

At the same time we are in this daily adoption hell, we go to Rani's and place an order for a houseful of new and antique furniture, all of it teak except for one beautiful rosewood desk. We've learned that our Paris apartment, unlike most diplomat housing abroad, will be unfurnished, which means we will be allotted a generous weight allowance for furniture when we get moved. We've also learned that our unfurnished Paris apartment will be twenty-five hundred square feet! Since we own almost no furniture, this seems like an opportune time to buy.

For two thousand dollars, we get an antique bookcase with glass doors, a coffee table and two matching end tables, two nightstands, a magnificent bedstead so solid I can do flips on my side without waking up Dana, a dining table and chairs for ten, a custom shoe cabinet, three antique dressers, an enormous china cabinet, an antique curio with lots of glass, a sideboard with rosewood inlay, a bunkbed, a dowry chest made of Burmese teak, and an unusual piece we call "piece of furniture" or "POF."

Before we can take them, all of the antiques have to be refinished and the new pieces have to be built using recycled wood from older, damaged pieces. We are assured all of this will be ready by our pack-out date a week before our departure. Rani's team has never built a bunkbed before. We show them a picture in a magazine and explain that the beds must be stackable and separable into two stand-alone twin beds. Rani's two most skilled carpenters refuse to make it.

"No, saar. Cannot do. Design unsafe."

This makes no sense to me. "Design unsafe?"

The carpenters converse at length.

"They have never heard of such a thing," Dinesh translates. "And they are afraid for safety of children."

After much time spent in persuasion, the carpenters finally agree to make a bunkbed that cannot be separated into two separate bunks. They won't budge at any price, so we do it their way. I figure I can someday have a carpenter cut it and finish it properly somewhere else. The bed is beautiful (for a bunkbed) when it's finished, but for some reason they have made it ten feet tall! The only room it can work in will have to have at least twelve-foot ceilings. (Luckily for us, our apartment in Paris turns out to have fifteen-foot ceilings.)

Our last month in India, Dinesh comes over after work every day to play with the children. He sits on the floor babbling to Nina until we have to ask him to go home. Since we don't hire a driver to replace him for our last few months, Dinesh feels it his duty to wash our car at least once a week. Finally, I stop protesting and just let him do it. Dinesh feels responsible for us being without a driver, and no amount of argument will change his attitude.

"You were never any good, Dinesh. We're better off without you," I tell him.

"Yes, saar. I know, saar." But he just keeps coming back.

Toward the end Dana and I are terribly busy with adoption-related issues, last-minute errands to run, farewell parties, and shopping trips. Dinesh insists on taking two weeks' leave from his new job to drive for us our last two weeks in India.

"Are you nuts? The Brits will fire you."

"It is already arrange, saar. They are giving me two weeks' paid leave."

I honestly don't know how we could've gotten everything done if we hadn't been able to rely on Dinesh again for those last days.

Finding ongoing employment for the rest of our staff is another item of major importance. I find work for our gardener, Narayanan, with another consulate family, and Kutti decides she will not work in order to take care of her mother. I am, however, having some trouble placing Shanthi, and time is running out. Finally, I convince a Singaporean friend from playgroup to hire her at the same salary. I breathe a sigh of relief. Thrilled that I have been able to do right by our servants, I happily present Shanthi with the good news.

"I don't want to work for Singapore's woman, saar. No."

"Why? It's a good job."

"No, saar. I want to work for American Consulate family."

"Shanthi, there's not another American family coming for three months."

"Then I wait, saar."

"Shanthi, you spent six months out of a job before I hired you. What if the new family coming doesn't hire you? Do you know how many cooks are looking for a job in Chennai?"

"I want to work for American family, saar."

"Shanthi, please, take the job and just quit if you get something better. What's wrong with that?"

"Saar, you the only master I work for who doesn't beat me or try to get 'sexical' with me. Americans are best people."

"No, Shanthi. There are tons of bad Americans. There are good people and bad people everywhere. And don't call me 'master.'"

"OK, saar," she says finally, with a curt, irritated head bobble. "You always right for me. I do what you say."

Our discussion has been at a pretty high volume, and we both walk our separate ways. I have never been so frustrated with her, and I think she probably feels the same.

Dinesh studies me and after a moment says, "You are looking like married couple, saar."

I glare at him. Then we burst out laughing.

❊❊❊

With less than two weeks to go, we *still* have no court date. I'm a madman not to be trifled with. Shanthi avoids me like the plague, and I can't be sure if Kutti even comes to work anymore. Dana and I agree that I will stay in India with Nina awaiting her paperwork. We discuss whether Cole should go to the US with Dana or stay with Nina and me in India. Dana has to begin six months of French-language training in Washington, DC, in short order, and Cole has to start school. To make things worse, after Dana's official departure date Nina and I can no longer stay in The Flame. Dinesh offers to let us live with him and his extended family. I begin to lose my mind.

"Money," I cry to Dana, pounding my forehead with the palm of my hand. "That's what they want. They want us to pay them off. Do you think that's what they want? We can't do that. And what if this never ends? I guess we'll just have to live in India forever. I swear, if and when we get out of here, I am never setting foot in this godforsaken country again!"

The phone rings. Our lawyer.

"Your court date is set for the day after tomorrow."

"I'll believe it when I see it."

"No, it is certain."

"Is it really set for the day after tomorrow or are you just telling us that?"

"It is official."

Ten days before we are scheduled to leave the country, a court in the neighboring state of Andhra Pradesh finally makes us Nina's legal guardians. I don't believe it until I get the documents in my hands. I'd like to say we celebrate in grand style, but we've been so stressed out with the whole mess that we don't feel anything but relief and an overwhelming desire to get on the next plane out of India. We can now apply for Nina's passport and take her home with us. She will be a US citizen within months, and a court in Texas will make her our legally adopted daughter by the end of the summer. She will become the only one of our children to receive a Texas birth certificate. All that's left for us now is to get our furniture from Rani's and leave.

How can we say good-bye to India? Despite the heat, dust, and disease; despite the utter chaos of it all; despite the inefficiencies, inconsistencies, and injustices, we have grown to love the place. Although our last several months have been occupied with pregnancy, ultrasounds, adoption woes, and just raising a family, we haven't wasted the opportunity to enjoy much of what India has to offer. Yet there are so many things left to see, and now we have no time.

So much has happened to our family in India. Our first child started kindergarten; we learned Dana could never conceive again only to find she can; Nina has joined our family, making India a part of us forever. Some of my grandchildren will be (at least) half Indian. I came to India with great job prospects, only to leave the corporate world altogether. We introduced Dana's parents to a new career in furniture sales that would for years bring them to India on their own, visiting our old friends and learning to love the country themselves. We made wonderful friends like Harish, Dinesh, Shanthi, and Rochelle, with whom we will remain in touch for many years. I learned to be patient when Indian drivers pull in front of our car with only inches to spare. When I now read the first chapters of this book, I marvel at my naïveté.

Cole, Nina, and I go to our last playgroup. I'm now leader of the group, and all my best friends are members. They make a nice cake for us and give me two books: *How to Talk to Your Kids about Sex* and *The Love Teachings of the Kama Sutra*. The latter has the inscription: "From the women of playgroup. Always think of us when you read this." Dana raises an eyebrow.

We are not at all surprised when, a week before the movers are due to arrive, we haven't received a stick of furniture from Rani's. I visit her almost daily to keep the pressure on but have given up believing they will actually finish on time. The furniture arrives, literally, as the movers place the last box from our house onto the truck. Rani's team unloads our furniture onto the street, and the movers wrap it up and place it directly into their van.

Our move itself is a classic Indian operation. Six workers and a manager spend six days packing our belongings. These men enter a room together, place the contents of all the drawers and cabinets on the floor, and silently wrap each item in great amounts of paper and tape before placing it gingerly in a box. In this way, a small item such as a saltshaker might become the size of a football when wrapped. Not one item gets broken, but, as I say, it takes them six days.

For five nights and six days, we must negotiate an increasingly complex maze of boxes to accomplish the simplest task in our home. Cole enjoys playing "fort" behind the boxes, stacked four high in our living room. Since the screen doors remain open all day as the movers go about their business, we are inundated with mosquitoes.

We have to unpack the mosquito nets from their boxes to get any sleep at night, and Dana and I huddle together on the couch each evening knocking mosquitoes out of the air with our electric tennis-racket-like mosquito swatters. This becomes something of a sport for us; we compete on body count. Since everything but our mosquito swatters and our beds is packed away, we only have two things to do at night, and we are much too tired for one of them.

When the movers finally get all of the boxes out of the house and sent away, we feel an exhilarating sense of liberation—not only because we can walk again but also because we realize we don't need all of the stuff. In a house with nothing but some lonely government furniture, the children play happily with each other, and Dana and I talk like we haven't in years. We won't see any of our new furniture and all but a few boxes of our belongings for half a year; since we will only be in Washington for six months, the department will put all our stuff in storage until we get to Paris.

The day before our departure, we go to the consulate for Dana's good-bye party. Visa seekers are made to wait in line for twenty more minutes while Dana stands in the consulate section surrounded by the American and Indian staff accepting fond farewells. The consul general makes a speech, the head of the consular section makes a speech, Dana makes a speech. Dana beams with pride as she is presented with a framed enlargement of a one-thousand-rupee bill with her face where Gandhi's is supposed to be. The antifraud section gives her a framed diploma from a fictitious Indian university stating she has graduated with honors in the discipline of "Soap and Detergents."

I watch Dana with mixed feelings, wishing I were the one receiving awards and the congratulations of my peers. At least I was able to pass the stupid exam on the third try, and now I'll get to be a US diplomat at long last—and a darn good one too. I hold Dana's awards and gifts for her as she shakes hands all round, I smile proudly as she gives her speech, and I carry everything home for her when they all get back to work. I'm happy to play this role, but I can't help wondering when it's going to be my time.

※ ※ ※

December is on the tail end of Chennai's annual rainy season, and this year has seen more rain than usual. This is one reason we had to wait so long for our furniture; the 100 percent humidity wouldn't allow the finish to dry. The few days before our departure are spectacularly beautiful, but on our last day, the rain comes down sideways in great sheets and fills the streets, which lack adequate drainage.

With nothing more to do, Shanthi, Kutti, Dinesh, and Narayanan sit together talking in the kitchen while we finish packing our suitcases. It is only at this moment I realize they will be going their separate ways as well. They are a good team that gets along well, and I guess they want to say good-bye to each other too. The four of them seem to genuinely like one another.

The phone rings. The torrential rain has reduced traffic to a standstill, and now we will have to leave an hour earlier for the airport. We scramble to get everything together. We pack right up until the time the consulate van comes for us. When we hear the car in the driveway, Dana and I march sadly downstairs to face the servants. We give packets of money to Shanthi, Kutti, and Narayanan, thanking them for two years of loyal service, and, as his lip trembles, I pay Dinesh for the previous two weeks of work.

Indian people don't hug. It's just not done. To them, it is a strange Western custom that is too intimate for friends and certainly for an employer-employee relationship. To me, our good-bye feels incomplete without one.

"Good-bye, saar," Shanthi says, a tear in her eye. "Thank you for everything."

"Good-bye, saar, madam," Kutti says, surprising us with speech. She bursts into tears.

Narayanan stands in the doorway, freshly showered, in his best lungi, grinning exuberantly. He waves enthusiastically and says "bye-bye" over and over again.

The phone rings. It is the consulate security chief. "You can't leave your car in the driveway."

I can barely hear him through the noise of the torrential downpour outside. We have already sold our Jeep, sight unseen, to an incoming American Consulate couple that has not yet arrived. We had planned to store it under our carport until the buyers arrived, and Dinesh promised he would start it for us every other day until the new family came. An American friend questioned the wisdom of leaving a set of keys with our former driver, but I trust Dinesh more than anyone I know.

"We're literally walking out the door now," I tell the security chief, irritated. "What are we going to do with it?"

"I don't know, but you can't leave your car in your driveway. I can't guarantee its safety."

"Any ideas what we can do we do with it?"

"You can't leave it in your driveway."

I hang up, call our friend Amanda, and explain our situation. She says we can leave the car in her garage. This involves a trip across town, and now we'll have to race against time to make our flight. As we herd the children into the consulate van, Shanthi, Kutti, and Narayan bid them an emotional farewell. Dana gets in the van with the kids, but I want to ride in the Jeep with Dinesh one last time. Dinesh drives us slowly and carefully to Amanda's with the consulate van following, and we park the Jeep in the garage. Amanda knows Dinesh well and has no qualms about him coming over anytime to check on the car.

I breathe a sigh of relief and turn to Dinesh; both of us are soaking wet from the downpour. He leans into the van and gives each of the children a kiss.

"Good-bye, saar. Good-bye, madam. Nina is very lucky to have you as parents."

"Thank you, Dinesh, but we are the lucky ones to have her," I say.

"I'll never forget you, saar, madam."

"We won't forget you, Dinesh," Dana says, and then we all begin to cry.

Dinesh gives us both great bear hugs, soaking Dana too, then turns away as we get in the van. After the driver closes the door, Dinesh stands in the rain and waves until we are out of sight.

We make good time to the airport despite the rain and are pleasantly surprised to find Harish waiting on us.

"We simply must have tea," he says in his characteristic rasp.

We join him in a greasy airport restaurant and discuss when we might meet again. We had been so wary of Harish in the beginning, but he never pressured Dana to do anything unethical or illegal with respect to visas for his friends or family. He turned out to be and remains one of our best friends.

In typical style, Harish loads us down with too many last-minute gifts and souvenirs for us to carry and shakes hands with Cole and Nina. The four of us ride the escalator in silence to our departure gate, waving to Harish in the crowd below. Finally, it is time to board, and everyone rushes at once for the door.

EPILOGUE

December 2013

LONG STORY, SHORT: I NEVER get to be a diplomat. I passed the exam on the third try, but the wheels of bureaucracy turn slowly. By the time I actually receive a job offer from the State Department, we are already preparing to leave Washington, DC, for Paris. Accepting the job would mean months of training for me at the Foreign Service Institute in Arlington, Virginia, and then an assignment to who-knows-where. We are faced with a stark choice: Dana has to give up her onward assignment to Paris, or I have to give up my dream of being a diplomat.

"It's your choice. I'll give up Paris for you," Dana says.

In the end, I choose Paris and my three babies—little Sam is born that March—over my dream career. I've gotten used to my role in our family, and I like it. I've never regretted that decision, but I can't help wondering what might have been.

✻✻✻

I live every day in Paris like a tourist, enjoying the city as if we might leave the next day. We enroll Cole in the excellent public school three doors from our apartment in the center of the city; he is fluent

GREGORY E. BUFORD

in French by Christmas. I carry Nina and Sam under my arms up and down the steps of the Paris Metro, we frolic with abandon in Jardin du Luxembourg, we stuff our double stroller onto crowded Paris buses on our way to a new playgroup, we hike to the top of Montmartre at least a dozen times, and we spin in circles under the Eiffel Tower. When we leave after two years, I've walked hundreds of miles in the city and know Paris like a tour guide.

During our three years in Phnom Penh, Cambodia, we check two more items off my bucket list: exploring Angkor Wat and floating the Mekong. Cole eats fried spiders in the market, and I build the kids a castle of bamboo that is the envy of the neighborhood. Nina and Sam join Cole at the French-language school, Lycée Français René Descartes, and we make side trips to Vietnam, Malaysia, Laos, Thailand, and Myanmar.

In Geneva, Switzerland, Dana's fourth assignment, we ski world-class slopes almost every weekend in winter, and in summer we ride the carousel and roll in the lush fire-ant-free grass in the Jardin Botanique. The children walk to school across a stone bridge over a creek in the woods. We hike the Alps between stunningly beautiful villages accessible only by cog railway. We drive the Mont Blanc tunnel into Italy and explore Tuscany, Naples, and, once more, the Amalfi Coast. My mother and father sell their home in Texas and move into an apartment attached to our Geneva home. It's the ideal situation; my parents had always wanted to be closer to their grandchildren, and I had always wanted it for them too. I'm also thrilled my parents have a unique opportunity to experience the beauty of Switzerland.

And then my mother gets cancer.

Dana resigns her position, and we go back to Texas; I can't bear being so far away from my mom, who has gone home for treatment. We try to become a normal family with normal friends. After eleven years in the slow lane, I go back to Dell and into the same job I had before we left. My colleagues at Dell have moved out of Austin and into the suburbs, had kids, and gotten older. Instead of lavish houseboat parties on Lake Travis or events where a Michael Dell stunt-double fast-ropes from a helicopter, we now have to pay for our own donuts; it is thoroughly depressing. Dana gets a job at the University of Texas, our children go to school in English, we move into a home that belongs to us and not the government, and we pay property taxes. No one wants to hear our tales of overseas adventures and the diplomat lifestyle. There is not automatically a community of new friends waiting for us as there had been in the Foreign Service. Normal is hard to handle.

Cole comes home from his first day of American middle school looking like a shell-shocked soldier.

"Well," I say, "how is school here different from school in Switzerland?"

"Different? There's not one single thing the same. And the food is disgusting."

In the sixth grade Nina comes to me for advice. "A kid asked me today, 'How come you're Mexican but you don't speak Spanish?' How do I respond to that?"

"Well, tell them, 'Thank you, but I'm from India. Do you want me to tell you about it?'"

We adjust. Nina becomes something of a softball superstar; Sam wins a speech contest and speaks in front of thousands at the University of Texas on Martin Luther King Day; we watch in stunned disbelief as Cole drives a motorized vehicle by himself. Dana and I long for the Foreign Service—the tight-knit foreign community in out-of-the way places, the excitement of moving to a new exotic locale every couple of years, the travel opportunities. It is hard to make friends in America; everyone is so busy. Essentially, we never recover from "reentry."

✹✹✹

India becomes our family's personal *hajj*: If we can afford it, we must one day show Nina from where she came. In elementary school Nina becomes fully aware of what it means to be adopted, and this realization is hard on her. She experiences nightmares of a biological family somewhere perishing in a fire. She wonders whose nose she has, whose eyes, whose lips. At times she cries, missing her unknown family, fantasizing that someday she might meet them.

"Isn't there some way we can find them?" she asks me at age ten. "Can't we go to India and look for them?"

My heart is splitting, but I have to be honest with her for her own good. "No, sweetheart. I'm sorry, but finding your biological family is impossible. There are more than a billion people in India, and all we have are their first names. You will never be able to find them."

"I can't believe," she sobs, utterly bereft, "that somewhere out there I have sisters that I will never meet."

That is a hard thing for a little girl to take. I show her the index fingerprints of her biological parents on the relinquishment document. She keeps a copy.

When Nina turns thirteen and Dana and I both have jobs, it is time to go back to India. We won't be traveling on diplomatic passports, and we will pay our own expenses, but we will make this trip of a lifetime. I go to lunch with Scott, my one friend who is interested.

"Well, we booked it. Our trip to India. We got our tickets yesterday," I tell him.

"Dude, I'd love to go to India with someone like you that knows his way around. That's like my dream come true. To travel."

"Nobody says 'dude' anymore."

"Hey, I got an idea," he says. "What if Melanie and I go with y'all?"

"Uh…"

"We'd just come along and do what y'all do. You'd hardly know we were there."

"Well…I guess…"

"Seriously? You think it could work?"

"Sure…hey, y'all want to have dinner on Sunday?"

I get a call from Scott later that afternoon.

"Hey, we're good to go."

"Cool," I say. "What time y'all want to come over?"

"Dude, I'm not talking about dinner. I'm talking about India. I've already got a travel agent working it up."

That night I have some explaining to do, and Nina is not a happy camper.

"This was my trip," she cries. "This trip was supposed to be about us going to India to see where I came from, not hanging out with your friends."

"Sorry. I never thought they would really come," I say lamely. "My bad."

✳✳✳

The seven of us arrive in Chennai to find the airport dramatically upgraded. Harish has sent two vans and drivers to collect us and our luggage, and Dinesh, our former chauffeur, is waiting with a smile. As I take in the sights and smells of India, I am bowled over by a wave of nostalgia that gives me goose bumps. Our Foreign Service days come back to me, and I am lost in thought. Feelings return—

being a foreigner again, observing a culture from the outside, comparing and contrasting everything to home, noticing the myriad differences and even more numerous similarities. I squeeze Dana's hand; she grins. Nina stares out the window of the van, her face inscrutable.

Dinesh is now a slightly chubby personification of the Indian dream. His parents arranged for him an excellent match to intelligent and kindhearted Dharani—Dana describes her as a "female Dinesh," intended as the most sincere of compliments. They have two beautiful girls—Harshini and Gaayathri—who call us "auntie" and "uncle" and entertain us with song and dance in their home. (After seeing how well Dinesh and Dharani made out, I'm a big fan of arranged marriages. Dharani and I are conspiring to arrange Sam's marriage to Gaayathri, but the kids don't know that yet. Well, I guess they do now...) Dinesh has worked his way up from driver to protocol assistant at the British Deputy High Commission. He spent a week in training in London in order to be the personal driver and assistant to Prince Charles and Camilla during their 2013 visit to India. Prince Charles personally commended Dinesh for his excellent work. Through hard work and careful saving, Dinesh and Dharani managed to buy a piece of property and build a home, which they remodeled into a three-story tenant-occupied dwelling. We visit their home, and Dharani cooks for us the best meal we eat during our two-week trip. (Find some of her recipes at gregorybuford.com.)

Shanthi, our former housekeeper and cook, has graduated from a hut of scrap wood to a cinder-block hovel complete with (unreliable) electricity and (non-potable) running water. She has reunited with Dom, her deadbeat husband, who had once threatened to jump from the roof of our home. Shanthi's daughter, Priya, has a cute baby of her own. Shanthi's sister, Selvi, our original housekeeper who greeted us at our home on our first night in India, is still yellow with turmeric and still smiling.

"God has blessed me truly, saar, that saar and madam and children come back to India," Shanthi cries. "Saar is looking exactly same, saar. Madam looking older."

We treat her extended family to lunch at Saravana Bhavan, a South Indian vegetarian chain restaurant, and a good time is had by all.

Harish has shifted more of the daily operation of his business to his son, Pranae, and spends time with us on every day of our visit. Each day he picks me up at dawn for a stop at his favorite tea shop and a walk on the beach. He still drives an unpretentious little piece of junk. He carries us to a Christmas service at Stella Maris College, where the nuns give us green plastic baby Jesuses and serve us tea.

"The people are just so nice here," Sam remarks. "It's like we're family."

If you wanted to write a comedic caricature of an ugly American tourist leaving a swath of ill will through a foreign country, you couldn't do a better job than to chronicle the trip of my friend Scott in South India. He hates every restaurant, berates every waiter, and is desperate for American fast-food in less than forty-eight hours on the ground.

"Believe it or not," I tell him, "you hate India now, but a few months after you get home you're going to want to come back. Just wait."

"Dude, no f%@&ing way."

Scott stands at the door of an ancient Hindu temple, an architectural masterpiece, and describes it as "disgusting superstition." He refuses to honor local custom and take off his shoes when entering our friends' homes and places of worship. We visit the former French enclave of Pondicherry—"a waste of time"—and stop at the famous experimental township of Auroville—"f%@&ing crazy hippie commune." A dinner party is held in our honor at the American consul general's home—the Adyar River still stinking in the background—and all our Indian friends will be there.

"Are there going to be any Muslims at this party?" Scott asks, "'cause I don't know how I feel about that."

"Well, if you don't like it, you are welcome to go back to your hotel," I tell him, wondering how we ever became friends.

He is ruining Nina's trip. "He keeps talking about how much he can't stand India and Indians," she says, "and, well, I'm Indian, and it's really starting to *make me mad!*"

I resolve to cut my ties with Scott and Melanie as soon as we get off the trip. When they tell us they want to leave early, Dana and I bend over backward to get them on a flight the next day.

❊❊❊

We take the overnight train—just to give the kids the experience—to visit Nina's orphanage in Hyderabad, and it's a big hit.

"This is just like the Hogwarts Express," Sam exclaims.

Sister Theresa, the nun who had showed faith in my ability to take care of an infant alone, greets us with hugs and kisses. Her mobility is somewhat diminished, but otherwise she is unchanged. The orphanage, however, is a shadow of its former self. Previously, it had been home to more than a hundred babies and children and full of life, but now only eighteen teenage girls live there. These girls had lost their parents in a monsoon that struck India's southeastern coast a few years earlier. Rooms that had once been full of toys and cribs are shuttered. Sister Theresa explains that the orphanage had stopped taking in small children years earlier because she had become unable to manage the operation, and none of the younger nuns was interested in taking over. Also, the regulatory regime became more difficult to navigate.

Nina is uncharacteristically speechless and smiles shyly as she is surrounded by girls her age who are a head shorter and a good deal thinner than she. The girls are fascinated by this stranger who appears Indian but is not like them in their *salwar kameez* and bangles. We don't speak a word of the local Telugu, but since the girls learn English in school, we are able to communicate with them. Most of the girls have no possibility of ever being adopted at their advanced age—they will be educated and become nuns, domestics, possibly computer programmers. One girl smiles and tells us she will soon be joining an adoptive American family in the Midwest.

Dana and I stare at Nina, watching her struggle to process the experience. She looks overwhelmed. Nina and the boys sit together with the orphans on the floor and play games.

After some time, Sister Theresa takes Nina into her office, and they talk privately for an hour. When they finally come out, it is clear many tears were shed.

"What did she say?" Dana asks.

"She says I'm very lucky to have such a wonderful family and that I need to appreciate you." She gives me and Dana a hug. "OK. We can go now."

All the hassle and expense of the trip is worth it for this moment. I look at Dana. She has tears in her eyes too. I take one last look at the orphanage, at Sister Theresa, at the remaining girls. I want to linger, but Nina is already down the stairs. She has moved on. Her nightmares of her biological family in peril cease and don't return.

The reader may recall my niece Tiffany visited us in India when she was twelve. The visit changed her life, and she dreamed of one day joining the Foreign Service like her Aunt Dana. Shortly after our return from India, Tiffany passes the Foreign Service exam on the second try—besting her Uncle Greg. On the last day of her basic training in Washington, DC, she waits on the edge of her seat with her new husband, Seth, as her country of assignment is announced.

Tiffany now lives in Chennai, India, the same place Dana went on her first tour of duty, paying her first-tour dues at the same visa window with much of the same local staff as Dana had fourteen years earlier. Dinesh, Dharani, Shanthi, and Harish were waiting for her when she arrived. That's just the way things are done in India.

✾✾✾

Scott apologizes, and I finally get over it. We remain friends. Three months after we return from India, I get a call.

"Dude, don't laugh, but I can't stop thinking about it. India, I mean. It's like I'm infected. At work they call me Mr. India. I got to go back there some day. Hey, you want to go get some Indian food for lunch?"

Infected. Like a virus. Living in India changed us forever. We went there in fear and learned to love it. And then hate it. And then love it again despite all its warts—like a good marriage. We reintroduced our children to India, and they fell in love with the people as we have. Returning to India helped Nina find some closure she needed that Dana and I would never have been able to provide.

At the same time, Dana and I had developed a rose-colored nostalgia for the expatriate life since returning to the US, and visiting India again reminded us that the grass is never as green as it appears; we are reminded of what it feels like to be foreign again, away from family and roots, dealing with the stresses of life in a developing country. We are so grateful we had the chance to live in India and be in the Foreign Service. The experience altered our perspective in ways difficult to express and that we had not anticipated. We found that we can't come home and see things the same way again—that we can't see America in isolation. And, at the end of the day, home is where you make it, and there's no place like home.

ACKNOWLEDGMENTS

I OWE A DEBT OF gratitude to a great number of people who helped with this book and encouraged me along the way. I wish to thank Dinesh, Shanthi, Kutti, Selvi, Narayanan, Heather, Leela, and Harish who took great care of us in India; the Virginia Bufords, who insisted I write this book; Tiffany Buford Burchett; Jennifer McIntyre, who hosted us in her home on our return to India; the women of the Chennai playgroup, for friendship and acceptance; Jennifer Spande; Kaushi and Captain G. Ramaswamy; Gaurav Bansal and family; my mother and father; my wife, Dana, who always laughs at my stupid jokes; the people of India, who are its saving grace.

About the Author

G REG BUFORD HAS LIVED IN Japan, India, France, Cambodia, and Switzerland. He's settled down (for the moment) in Austin, Texas, with his wife, Dana, and their children. He published his first novel, *Making Ghosts Dance*, in 2017. Kept: An American Househusband in India is his first work of nonfiction. Learn more and see images of India at gregorybuford.com.

Made in the USA
Monee, IL
13 December 2020